Righteous Through Faith

A Study of the
Epistle to the Romans

By
Armin J. Panning

 Multi-Language Publications
Bringing the Word to the World

The original text is produced by Multi-Language Publications of the Wisconsin Evangelical Lutheran Synod.

Copyright © 2011

Printed in 2011
Reprinted in 2015

ISBN 1-931891-35-4

Level Two, Book 2

TABLE OF CONTENTS

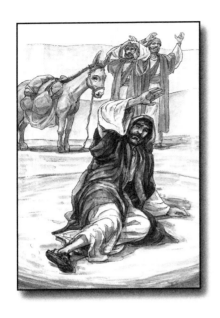

RIGHTEOUS
THROUGH FAITH

Righteous Through Faith:
A Study of the Epistle to the Romans

SECTION ONE:
Introduction to Romans

Read Romans 1:1 (chapter 1, verse 1)

[1] I, Paul, am writing this letter. I serve Christ Jesus. I have been appointed to be an apostle. God set me apart to tell others his good news.

According to ancient letter writing custom, the author of a letter named himself at the beginning of the letter. Here the author calls himself Paul, but that was not always his name. Originally his name was Saul.

Saul belonged to a very strict Jewish group that did not accept Jesus as the promised Messiah (He was also called Christ, Jesus, Lord, and Savior). Saul thought followers of Christ (Christians) were dangerous and should be destroyed. When Stephen, the first Christian martyr, was stoned to death, Saul was on the scene. After that he often raided homes in Jerusalem and arrested Christian men and women.

Once he was on a raid to arrest Christians in the distant city of Damascus. On the road, Jesus blocked his path and knocked him to the ground. "Saul, Saul, why are you persecuting me?" Jesus demanded. Now Saul knew it was wrong to persecute Christians. Instead of persecuting Christians, Saul now accepted God's assignment to preach the Christian message to people. That is why he can say, "I serve Christ Jesus."

Jesus appointed him to be an apostle. An apostle is someone who is sent out to share a message. God set him apart to preach and teach the good news about Christ. As a Christian missionary Saul changed his name to Paul.

The stoning of Stephen.

Saul meets Jesus on the road to Damascus.

Things to remember:

1. The author of the letter to the Romans first had the name _____ but he changed it to _____.
2. Saul thought Christians were _____ and should be _____.
3. Saul arrested Christian men and women in _____ and even traveled to the city of _____.
4. On the road to Damascus Jesus met Saul and said to him "Why are you _____ me?"
5. Now Saul knew it was wrong to _____ Christians.
6. Jesus appointed Saul to be an _____.
7. An apostle is someone who is _____ to share a _____.
8. Paul's message was the _____ _____ about _____.

(Check your answers on page 12.)

Good News about God's Son

(Read Romans 1:2-4)

God set me apart to tell others his good news. [2] He promised the good news long ago. He announced it through his prophets in the Holy Scriptures.
[3] The good news is about God's Son. As a human being, the Son of God belonged to King David's family line. [4] By the power of the Holy Spirit, he was appointed to be the mighty Son of God because he rose from the dead. He is Jesus Christ our Lord.

An apostle is someone sent out to share a message. He does not bring his own message. He shares the message of the one who sent him. Paul writes, "God: set me apart to tell others his good news." It is God's message that the apostle Paul shares—and it is good news. It is "the good news about God's Son."

The first promise of this good news came many years ago. In fact, it came soon after creation. Adam and Eve fell into sin and should have suffered forever in hell for their disobedience. But God promised Eve that from her descendants a savior would be born. You can read about this promised "Seed of the woman" in Genesis 3:15, the first book of the Bible.

God repeated this promise of a savior to the patriarchs Abraham, Isaac, and Jacob (ancestors of the Jewish nation). After that God sent many prophets, such as Isaiah and Jeremiah, to repeat the message for their hearers and also to write it down in the Old Testament Scriptures for future generations. After many years the promised "Seed of the woman" was born of the virgin Mary, a descendant of King David. Thus Jesus of Nazareth, born of Mary, was truly human.

But Jesus is more than just a man. He is also the Son of God. Isaiah gave him the name Immanuel, which means, "God with us." (Read Isaiah 7:14) How can we be sure that he is more than a man—that he is also true God? He was born without a human father—"by the power of the Holy Spirit," as Paul says. What is more, he did what no human could have done. He rose from the dead.

By faith in him, this "mighty Son of God" is also our Lord.

Things to remember:

9. God sent Paul out to tell others of his _____
   _____.

10. The good news is about _____ _____.

11. After the fall into sin God promised Eve that from her descendants a _____ would be born.

12. God repeated this promise of a savior to the
    _____.

God makes a plan to save us.

13. The _____ wrote down the promise in the Old Testament Scriptures.

14. The promised "Seed of the woman" was _____ who was born of _____. Therefore Jesus is truly _____.

15. Jesus had no _____ father. He was born by the power of the _____ _____. Thus he was true _____ as well as true man.

(Check your answers on page 12.)

A Gift from God

(Read Romans 1:5)

[5] I received God's grace because of what Jesus did so that I could bring glory to him. He made me an apostle to all those who aren't Jews. I must invite them to have faith in God and obey him.

Grace is a beautiful word that has two meanings. Sometimes it talks about God's love that moves him to give us gifts. Sometimes "grace" refers to the gift itself. Here Paul tells us, "I received a *gift* from God."

The gift was that God made him an apostle. As an apostle, Paul could glorify God by sharing God's promised savior with the people God sent him to. These people were "those who aren't Jews." Usually we call them Gentiles.

Paul's message was that the Old Testament promise of a savior was not just for Jews, but for all people. That is why he could invite Gentiles also "to have faith in God."

Things to remember:

16. Sometimes grace means God's _____ for us. At other times it refers to the _____ God gives us.

17. Paul's gift was that God made him an _____.

18. As an apostle, Paul could glorify God by _____

_____.

19. The people God sent Paul to were not Jews but

_____.

(Check your answers on page 12.)

The Receivers of Paul's Letter

(Read Romans 1:6,7)

[6] You also are among those who are appointed to belong to Jesus Christ.
[7] I am sending this letter to all of you in Rome who are loved by God and appointed to be his people. May God our Father and the Lord Jesus Christ give you grace and peace.

In ancient letter writing first the author tells who he is. Then he says whom he is writing to. Here Paul tells us this letter is addressed to believers in Rome. As a fellow believer Paul prays that God would give them the gift of peace.

Things to remember:
20. The writer of this letter is _____.
21. He is sending the letter to people in _____.
22. His readers are fellow-_____.
(Check your answers on page 12.)

Paul Wants to Visit Rome

(Read Romans 1:8-15)

[8] First, I thank my God through Jesus Christ for all of you. People all over the world are talking about your faith. [9] I serve God with my whole heart. I preach the good news about his Son. God knows that I always remember you [10] in my prayers. I pray that now at last it may be God's plan to open the way for me to visit you.
[11] I long to see you. I want to make you strong by giving you a gift from the Holy Spirit. [12] I want us to cheer each other up by sharing our faith.

[13] Brothers and sisters, I want you to know that I planned many times to visit you. But until now I have been kept from coming. My work has produced results among others who are not Jews. In the same way, I want to see results among you.
[14] I have a duty both to Greeks and to non-Greeks. I have a duty both to wise people and to foolish people. [15] So I really want to preach the good news also to you who live in Rome.

Paul did not start the Christian congregation in Rome. In fact, he has not yet been there. But he very much wants to visit them. Every day he prays for them and for himself, asking that God will let him visit these believers in Rome.

Paul's reason for wanting to visit the Romans is to preach the good news of the Savior to them. They already are believers, but through this message the Holy Spirit will make their faith even stronger. Here too Paul expects something for himself, namely, that his own faith will grow while sharing the message.

The reason Paul has not been able to come to Rome sooner is that he has been very busy preaching to others. This preaching enjoyed good success both among "Greeks and non-Greeks," among "wise people and foolish people." In other words, Paul shares his message with everyone who will listen.

Things to remember:

23. Paul did not _____ the congregation in Rome but he very much wants to __ _____ them.
24. Paul's purpose for coming to Rome is to _____ the good news of the gospel to them.
25. Through this preaching of the good news the Holy Spirit will _____ their faith.
26. The reason Paul has not visited the Romans earlier is that he has been very busy _____ to others.
27. Paul can preach to others because the good news is a message for _____.

(Check your answers on page 12.)

Righteous through Faith

(Read Romans 1:16,17)

¹⁶ I am not ashamed of the good news. It is God's power. And it will save everyone who believes. It is meant first for the Jews. It is meant also for those who aren't Jews.
¹⁷ The good news shows how God makes people right with himself. From beginning to end, becoming right with God depends on a person's faith. It is written, "Those who are right with God will live by faith."— (*Habakkuk 2:4*)

An apostle brings the message of the one who sent him. Paul is God's apostle. His message has God's power. It will save everyone who believes it, both Jews and Gentiles. For this reason Paul can boldly preach the good news of the gospel to anyone.

Remember that Jesus Christ is true God and true man. As true God he came down to earth to be our substitute. That means in our place he kept all of God's commandments that we should have kept. By his perfect life he earned righteousness for sinners.

The wages of sin is death. All people are sinners. All deserve to die and suffer eternally in hell. But as true man Jesus died in the sinner's place. He paid the punishment we deserved.

By his perfect life in our place and by his innocent death for us Christ has earned righteousness. The good news Paul has to share with the Romans (and us) is that God has accepted Christ's righteousness as the sinner's righteousness, if only the sinner believes it. It is not that the sinner becomes righteous. Rather, with their sins forgiven through faith in what Christ has done, God now looks at believers as if they were holy. God declares them righteous. It is like a judge declaring a criminal innocent.

Being right with God through faith in Christ has always been God's plan of salvation. It was the plan already in the Old Testament, as the quotation from the prophet Habakkuk shows.

Things to remember:

28. Paul can boldly preach the gospel because it is a message for _____.
29. As true God, Christ came to earth to be our
_____.
30. Christ perfectly kept all of the _____.
31. By keeping the commandments, Jesus earned
_____ for sinners.
32. This righteousness comes to the sinner through
_____ in Christ.
33. As true man, Christ died an innocent death. By his death he suffered the death that _____ should have suffered.
34. "Being right with God" does not mean that sinners actually _____ righteous. Rather, with their sins forgiven in Christ, God looks at believers as if they were _____. He _____ them righteous.
35. Throughout history, the only way of salvation has always been through _____ in Christ.
(Check your answers on page 12.)

Things to remember-Answers
1. Saul, Paul; 2. dangerous, destroyed; 3. Jerusalem, Damascus; 4. persecuting; 5. persecute; 6.apostle; 7.sent, message; 8. good news, Christ; 9. good news; 10. God's son; 11. savior; 12. patriarchs; 13. prophets; 14. Jesus, Mary, human; 15. human, Holy Spirit, God; 16. love, gifts; 17. apostle; 18. sharing the message of God's promised Savior; 19. Gentiles; 20. Paul, 21. Rome; 22. believers; 23. start, visit; 24. preach; 25. strengthen; 26. preaching; 27. everyone; 28. everyone; 29. substitute; 30. commandments; 31. righteousness; 32. faith; 33. sinners; 34. become, righteous, declares; 35. faith.

TEST - Righteous Through Faith: A Study of the Epistle to the Romans

Section 1
Please review the "Things to remember."

---

1. The author of the letter to the Romans first had the name _____ but he changed it to _____.

2. Saul thought Christians were _____ and should be _____.

3. On the road to Damascus Jesus met Saul and said to him, "Why are you _____ me?"

4. Jesus appointed Saul to be an _____.

5. After the fall into sin God promised Eve that from her descendants a _____ would be born.

6. This promised "Seed of the woman" was _____ who was born of _____. Hence Jesus is truly _____.

7. Jesus had no earthly father. He was born by the power of the _____ _____. Thus he is also true _____.

8. Most of the people Paul preached to were not Jews but _____.

9. Paul did not start the congregation in Rome but he very much wanted to _____ them.

10. Paul's purpose for coming to Rome was to _____ the good news of the gospel to them.

11. By keeping all the commandments, Jesus as true God earned _____ for sinners.

12. As true man, Christ died an innocent death. By his death he suffered the death that _____ should have suffered.

13. With their sins forgiven in Christ, God looks at believers as if they were _____.

14. Throughout history, the only way of salvation has always been through _____ in Christ.

(Check your answers on page 192.)

RIGHTEOUS
THROUGH FAITH

SECTION 2:
All People are Sinners

Romans 1:18 - 3:20

Righteous Through Faith:
A Study of the Epistle to the Romans

SECTION TWO:
All People are Sinners

Sinners Have No Excuse

(Read Romans 1:18-20)

[18] God shows his anger from heaven. It is against all the godless and evil things people do. They are so evil that they say no to the truth. [19] The truth about God is plain to them. God has made it plain.
[20] Ever since the world was created it has been possible to see the qualities of God that are not seen. I'm talking about his eternal power and about the fact that he is God. Those things can be seen in what he has made. So people have no excuse for what they do.

Sinners cannot plead ignorance. When they look at the created world around them, they know that someone very powerful has made it and controls it. They can see his eternal power and they know that he is God. Creatures owe obedience to their Creator God. When they do godless and evil things, they are saying "NO" to God. They are sinning. This makes our holy God very angry.

Things to remember:
1. People can tell from _____ that there is a God.
2. People owe _____ to their Creator God.
3. When people do not obey God they are _____.
(Check your answers on page 31.)

Gentiles Are Sinners (Romans 1:21-2:16)

(Read Romans 1:21-25)

The creation of the world.

[21] They knew God. But they didn't honor him as God. They didn't thank him. Their thinking became worthless. Their foolish hearts became dark. [22] They claimed to be wise. But they made fools of themselves. [23] They would rather have statues of gods than the glorious God who lives forever. Their statues of gods are made to look like people, birds, animals and reptiles.

[24] So God let them go. He allowed them to do what their sinful hearts wanted to. He let them commit sexual sins. They polluted one another's bodies by what they did.

[25] They chose a lie instead of God's truth. They worshiped and served created things. They didn't worship the Creator. But he must be praised forever. Amen.

In this section Paul is speaking to Gentiles. He will be addressing his Jewish readers in the next section.

For the Gentiles to see God's power and eternity in creation but then to choose not to worship him was foolish. That however is what the Gentiles did. Instead of worshipping the Creator, they sinned by worshipping his creatures. They made idols for themselves of wood, stone or precious metal. To worship statues looking like people, birds, animals, or reptiles was an insult to the true God who deserves to be praised forever.

Things to remember:

4. Paul is here speaking to _____.
5. The Gentiles sinned by _____ _____.
6. Worshipping an idol is an _____ to the true God.

(Check your answers on page 31.)

(Read Romans 1:26-28)

[26] So God let them go. They were filled with shameful longings. Their women committed sexual acts that were not natural. [27] In the same way, the men turned away from their natural love for women. They burned with sexual longing for each other. Men did shameful things with other men. They suffered in their bodies for all the twisted things they did.

[28] They didn't think it was important to know God. So God let them go. He allowed them to have dirty minds. They did things they shouldn't do.

God does not force people to do things. When sinners decide to do bad things, God lets them. That is what happened with the Gentiles Paul is describing. They rebelliously made themselves guilty of homosexuality.

Sexuality is a gift from a gracious creator God. It is a natural impulse that draws men and women together. It is God's way of populating the world and continuing the human race. But the gay community among the Gentiles did not respect God's way. Many chose same-gender sex. Paul is very plain: "Their women committed sexual acts that were not natural. In the same way, the men turned away from their natural love for women. They burned with sexual longing for each other. Men did shameful things with other men."

Such wickedness does not escape God's notice. Just as today a promiscuous lifestyle leads to the spread of social diseases and HIV complications, so the Gentiles of Paul's day "suffered in their bodies for all the twisted things they did."

<u>Things to remember:</u>
7. If sinners decide to do bad things, God _____
   _____ .
8. Sexuality is a _____ from God.
9. Many Gentiles spoiled God's gift by choosing
   _____ _ _ sex.
(Check your answers on page 31.)

(Read Romans 1:29-32)

[29] They are full of every kind of sin, evil and ungodliness. They want more than they need. They commit murder. They want what belongs to other people. They fight and cheat. They hate others. They say mean things about other people. [30] They tell lies about them. They hate God. They are rude and proud. They brag. They think of new ways to do evil.

They don't obey their parents. [31] They are foolish. They can't be trusted. They are not loving and kind.

[32] They know that God's commands are right. They know that those who do evil things should die. But they continue to do those very things. They also approve of others who do them.

Homosexuality is a serious sin, but it is by no means the only sin. Paul may have highlighted same-gender sex in the previous verses because it is so evident that it is an unnatural activity. Paul now goes on to name a lot of other sins, all of which seem much more natural for people to do. There may be a little overlap in the actions Paul describes, but there are many separate sins Paul names in his list. All of them are "evil things" for which the sinner should die.

Not only do sinners do these things themselves, but they wickedly encourage others to join them. To return for a moment to the gay community, note that today many homosexuals not only make a point of announcing their own "coming out of hiding" but they encourage others to do the same.

Things to remember:
10. Paul also mentions many non-sexual sins. Name some of them _____ _____.
11. For doing such things Gentiles should

_____ _____.

12. Doing such sins is serious, but it is even worse when sinners _____ others to do the same.

(Check your answers on page 31.)

God Judges Fairly

(Read Romans 2:1-11)

[1] If you judge someone else, you have no excuse for it. When you judge another person, you are judging yourself. You do the same things you blame others for doing.

[2] We know that when God judges those who do evil things, he judges fairly. [3] Though you are only a human being, you judge others. But you yourself do the same things. So how do you think you will escape when God judges you?

[4] Do you make fun of God's great kindness and favor? Do you make fun of God when he is patient with you? Don't you realize that God's kindness is meant to turn you away from your sins?

[5] But you are stubborn. In your heart you are not sorry for your sins. You are storing up anger against yourself. The day of God's anger is coming. Then his way of judging fairly will be shown. [6] God "will give to each person in keeping with what he has done."—(*Psalm 62:12; Proverbs 24:12*)

[7] God will give eternal life to those who keep on doing good. They want glory, honor, and life that never ends. [8] But there are others who only look out for themselves. They don't accept the truth. They go down an evil path. God will pour out his burning anger on them. [9] There will be trouble and suffering for everyone who does evil. That is meant first for the Jews. It is also meant for the non-Jews. [10] But there will be glory, honor and peace for everyone who does good. That is meant first for the Jews. It is also meant for the non-Jews. [11] God treats everyone the same.

People are quick to judge others and suggest what the punishment for their evil deeds should be. But that is a big mistake. Because the one doing the judging is himself a sinner and also does evil things, he is calling for punishment on himself.

The one doing the judging deserves to be punished because he is actually blaming God. He misunderstands God's patience. He blames God for waiting so long and not dealing harshly with the sinner. In reality God is just giving the sinner time to repent. Eventually there will be just judgment for all.

There is a definite standard by which God judges, but we have to be very careful that we do not misunderstand how Paul describes it here. He writes: "God will give eternal life to those who keep on doing good… But there are others who only look out for themselves. They don't accept the truth. They go down an evil path."

The lost son confesses his sins to his father.

It could sound as though salvation is earned by doing good, but that is not true. Later in the letter Paul will explain more fully that salvation is purely by faith in Christ, by trusting in the merit Christ has won. That important truth is included here. Note that Paul says God will give eternal life. It is a gift that is given to believers. The others Paul speaks of are unbelievers. They "don't accept the truth" of Christ having done everything for them. As a result they don't have the love and appreciation that leads believers to do good. Unbelievers do not produce the fruits of faith.

Things to remember:

13. The person judging others is actually judging _____, because he does the same sins.
14. God is patient with sinners in order to give them time to _____.
15. Salvation is not earned by doing _____ _____. It comes through _____ in what Christ has done.
16. Eternal life is a _____ that God gives to believers.

(Check your answers on page 31.)

(Read Romans 2:12-16)

[12] Some people do not know God's law when they sin. They will not be judged by the law when they die. Others do know God's law when they sin. They will be judged by the law. [13] Hearing the law does not make a person right with God. People are considered to be right with God only when they obey the law.

[14] Those who aren't Jews do not have the law. Sometimes they just naturally do what the law requires. They are a law for themselves. This is true even though they don't have the law. [15] They show that what the law requires is written on their hearts. The way their minds judge them gives witness to that fact. Sometimes their thoughts find them guilty. At other times their thoughts find them not guilty.

[16] People will be judged on the day God appoints Jesus Christ to judge their secret thoughts. That's part of my good news.

When Paul says, "Some people do not know God's law when they sin" he is speaking of non-Jews, the Gentiles. Gentiles were not under the Mosaic Law. Through Moses God on Mount Sinai gave special rules to the Jews, his chosen people. God's purpose was to set the Jewish nation apart because the Savior of the world was to come from them.

The Gentiles were not under the Mosaic Law, so they were not required to keep those special rules, but they still sinned. They sinned when they went against what they knew was God's will. By nature, people have a conscience. It tells them the difference between right and wrong. Paul says that even without the Mosaic Law "they (Gentiles) show that what the law requires is written on their hearts." People know it is wrong to hate and to envy, to steal and to kill. When they do such things, even though they know better, they are sinning. They deserve to be punished. Paul warns, "They will be judged on the day God appoints Jesus Christ to judge their secret thoughts." Gentiles need help, but so do the Jews.

Things to remember:

17. _____ were not under the Mosaic Law, but they had a different law. This law was written in their

_____.

18. By nature, people have a _____. When they go against their conscience they are

_____.

19. Sinners will be _____.

(Check your answers on page 31.)

Jews are Sinners (Romans 2:17–3:8)

(Read Romans 2:17–24)

[17] Suppose you call yourself a Jew. You trust in the law. You brag that you are close to God. [18] You know what God wants. You agree with what is best because the law teaches you. [19] You are sure you can lead people

God gives Moses the Ten Commandments.

who are blind. You are sure you are a light for those who are in the dark.
[20] You claim to be able to teach foolish people. You can even teach babies.
You think that in the law you have all knowledge and truth.
[21] You teach others. But you don't teach yourself! You preach against
stealing. But you steal! [22] You say that people should not commit adultery.
But you commit adultery! You hate statues of gods. But you rob temples!
[23] You brag about the law. But when you break it, you rob God of his
honor! [24] It is written, "Those who aren't Jews say evil things against
God's name because of you."—(*Isaiah 52:5; Ezekiel 36:22*)

Paul has clearly pointed out that the Gentiles' sexual
activity and other kinds of bad behavior were sins. He now
turns to his Jewish readers. On the outside, the Jewish nation
did not look as bad as their Gentile neighbors. But the Jews
had their own sins.

One was pride. God had chosen the Jews as the people
from whom the Savior would be born. He gave them special
rules to keep them separate from other nations. Because they
were a special nation, the Jews easily came to believe they
were better than others. Paul tells them "You brag that you
are close to God." But they did not realize that because of
their sins they really were not close to their holy God at all.

A second common sin among Jews was hypocrisy. They
told other people what not to do, but then they did these
things themselves. For example, they told others not to steal,
but then they themselves stole. In this way God was
dishonored. Even the Gentiles saw it and said evil things
against God's name. Thus the Jews were just as guilty as the
Gentiles.

Things to remember:
20. Two sins common among the Jews were
_____ and _____.
21. The Jews were proud because they were God's
_____ people.

22. Because the Jews did not practice what they preached, even the _____ spoke evil about the Jews' God.

(Check your answers on page 31.)

(Read Romans 2:25-29)

[25] Circumcision has value if you obey the law. But if you break the law, it is just as if you hadn't been circumcised.

[26] Sometimes those who aren't circumcised do what the law requires. Won't God accept them as if they had been circumcised? [27] Many are not circumcised physically, but they obey the law. They will prove that you are guilty. You are breaking the law, even though you have the written law and are circumcised.

[28] A man is not a Jew if he is a Jew only on the outside. And circumcision is more than just something done to the outside of a man's body.

[29] No, a man is a Jew only if he is a Jew on the inside. And true circumcision means that the heart has been circumcised. It is done by the Holy Spirit. It is more than just obeying the written Law. Then a man's praise will not come from others. It will come from God.

Because God had chosen the Jewish nation as the people from whom Jesus, the promised Savior, would be born, he made a special agreement, a covenant, with the Jews. By being circumcised, a Jew stated that he agreed with the covenant God had made with his people. However, if circumcised Jews did not do what God's covenant asked of them, they were actually denying the value of their circumcision.

On the other hand, if in faith an uncircumcised Gentile accepted God's covenant, which promised him a Savior, he was acceptable to God, even without being circumcised.

St. Paul points out that circumcision is something outward. What is vitally important is something inside a person, faith in the heart. This faith or trust in God's promise is given by the Holy Spirit. It is a gift, not something earned by doing. Such faith has God's "praise" or approval.

Things to remember:

23. God made a special _____ with the Jewish nation because _____ was to be born of them.

24. By being circumcised a Jew _____ _____ the covenant.

25. God's covenant with the Jews was open also to _____.

26. True circumcision is not outward but rather in a believer's _____.

27. Faith is a _____ given by the _____ _____.

(Check your answers on page 31.)

(Read Romans 3:1-4)

[1] Is there any advantage in being a Jew? Is there any value in being circumcised?

[2] There is great value in every way! First of all, the Jews have been given the very words of God.

[3] What if some Jews did not believe? Will the fact that they don't have faith keep God from being faithful? [4] Not at all! God is true, even though every human being is a liar. It is written,

"You are right when you sentence me.
You are fair when you judge me."—(*Psalm 51:4*)

If not only circumcised Jews but also uncircumcised Gentiles can be saved by faith in the promised Savior, is there any advantage for Jews to be special people under God's covenant? Paul says, "Yes there is!" God through Moses and the prophets gave the chosen people his written word, the Old Testament.

There have been, and always will be, some who do not accept God's Word. Does that make God any less reliable? Paul says, "Not at all" The psalmist is correct when he says God is "right" and "fair" in all he does.

Paul now in verses 5-8 addresses a point that a "human way of thinking" might raise against God's fairness:

5 Doesn't the fact that we are wrong prove more clearly that God is right? Then what can we say? Can we say that God is not fair when he brings his anger down on us? As you can tell, I am just using human ways of thinking. 6 God is certainly fair! If he weren't, how could he judge the world?

7 Someone might argue, "When I lie, it becomes clearer that God is truthful. It makes his glory shine more brightly. Why then does he find me guilty of sin?"

8 Why not say, "Let's do evil things so that good things will happen"? Some people actually lie by reporting that this is what we say. They are the ones who should be found guilty.

Human logic says, "When sinful people are shown to be wrong, God's holiness appears the more clearly. That is a benefit to God. Should he punish the sinner for that?"

Paul goes on to quote another terribly wrong suggestion that some false teachers were blaming on him. They misunderstood his teaching of grace as allowing the suggestion: "Let's do evil things so that good things will happen." Paul says simply: God's fairness will be seen clearly when they are found guilty on judgment day.

Things to remember:

28. The Jews enjoyed a great advantage because through Moses and the prophets God gave them _____

_____ _____ _____.

29. Paul says God is _____ when he punishes sinners.

(Check your answers on page 31.)

All People are Sinners (Romans 3:9-20)

(Read Romans 3:9)

9 What should we say then? Are we Jews any better? Not at all! We have already claimed that Jews are sinners. The same is true of those who aren't Jews.

Paul was a Jew, and some of the readers of this letter were Jews. Paul asks, "Are we any better?" Then he answers his own question: "Not at all! We have already claimed that Jews are sinners." And Gentiles are no better. Recall their disgusting sexual sins and other evils spoken of in chapter one. All people are sinners.

(Read Romans 3:10-18)

10 It is written,
  "No one is right with God, no one at all.
    11 No one understands.
    No one trusts in God.
12 All of them have turned away.
    They have all become worthless.
  No one does anything good,
      no one at all."—(*Psalms 14:1-3; 53:1-3; Ecclesiastes 7:20*)
13 "Their throats are like open graves.
    With their tongues they tell lies."—(*Psalm 5:9*)
  "The words from their lips are like the poison of a snake."—(*Psalm 140:3*)

    14 "Their mouths are full of curses and bitterness."—(*Psalm 10:7*)

15 "They run quickly to commit murder.

    16 They leave a trail of failure and pain.
17 They do not know the way of peace."—(*Isaiah 59:7,8*)

    18 "They don't have any respect for God."—(*Psalm 36:1*)

Ever since Adam and Eve's fall into sin, every one of their descendants has been infected with sin. Six times in verses 10-12 Paul says <u>no one</u> is acceptable before God. Twice in verse 12 he says <u>all</u> have become bad. This is supported by the many Scripture passages he quotes, mostly from the Psalms.

(Read Romans 3:19,20)

[19] What the law says, it says to those who are ruled by the law. Its purpose is to shut every mouth and make the whole world accountable to God. [20] So it can't be said that anyone will be made right with God by obeying the law. Not at all! The law makes us more aware of our sin.

The law is that part of God's Word that tells us what a holy God expects of us. Because we sinners cannot do what God's law demands, the law cannot make us right with God. It has a different purpose. It makes us aware of our sin. It shows us our need of a savior.

Things to remember:
30. How many people are sinners? _____
31. God's law tells us what God _____.
32. Because sinners can't keep the law, the law can't make us _____ with God.
33. The purpose of the law is to

_____.

(Check your answers on page 31.)

Things to remember-Answers
1. the created world; 2. obedience; 3. sinning; 4. Gentiles; 5. worshipping creatures; 6. insult; 7. let's them; 8. gift; 9. same-gender; 10. murder, fight, cheat, hate; 11. die; 12. encourage; 13. himself; 14. repent; 15. good works, faith; 16. gift; 17. Gentiles, hearts; 18. conscience, sinning; 19. punished; 20. pride, hypocrisy; 21. special; 22. Gentiles; 23. agreement, Jesus; 24. agreed with; 25. Gentiles; 26. heart; 27. gift, Holy Spirit; 28. the Old Testament Bible; 29. fair; 30. all; 31. expects of us; 32. right; 33. shows us our need for a savior.

Section 2

Please review the "Things to remember."

1. People can tell from _____ _____
    _____ that there is a God.

2. People owe _____ to their Creator God.

3. When people do not obey God they are _____.

4. Sexuality is a gift from God. Many Gentiles spoiled
    God's gift by choosing _____ sex.

5. For doing such things Gentiles should _____.

6. Doing such sins is serious, but it is even worse when
    sinners _____ others to do the same.

7. God is patient with sinners in order to give them time to
    _____.

8. Salvation is not earned by doing _____ _____.
    It comes through _____ in what Christ has done .

9. Eternal life is a _____ that God gives to
    believers.

10. _____ were not under the Mosaic law, but
    they had a different law. This law was written in their
    _____.

11. By nature, people have a _____. When they go against their conscience they are

    _____.

12. Two sins common among the Jews were pride and hypocrisy. The Jews were proud because they were God's _____ people.

13. God made a special _____ with the Jewish nation because _____ was to be born of them.

14. The Jews enjoyed a great advantage because through Moses and the prophets God gave them _____

    _____.

15. God's law tells us what God _____

    _____ _____. Because sinners can't keep the law, the law can't _____ _____.

16. The purpose of the law is to

    _____.

(Check your answers on page 192.)

RIGHTEOUS
THROUGH FAITH

SECTION 3:
Sinners are Justified or Forgiven

Romans 3:21 – 5:21

Righteous Through Faith:
A Study of the Epistle to the Romans

SECTION THREE:
Sinners are Justified or Forgiven

Righteous through Jesus Christ (Romans 3:21-31)

(Read Romans 3:21-22)

> [21] But now God has shown us how to become right with him. The Law and the Prophets give witness to this. It has nothing to do with obeying the law. [22] We are made right with God by putting our faith in Jesus Christ. That happens to all who believe.

Section Two ended on a very discouraging note. It told us that all people are sinners. None of us are right with God. Section Three begins with the very important word <u>but</u>. We have no righteousness, BUT there is a solution for our problem. It is spelled out in the Bible ("the Law and the Prophets"). It is a plan totally different from what we would have thought. We would have thought we have to keep God's law to get right with him. But God's plan has nothing to do with our doing anything. It has everything to do with what Jesus Christ has done for us.

(Read Romans 3:22b-25)

> It is no different for the Jews than for anyone else. [23] Everyone has sinned. No one measures up to God's glory. [24] The free gift of God's grace makes all of us right with him. Christ Jesus paid the price to set us free. [25] God gave him as a sacrifice to pay for sins. So he forgives the sins of those who have faith in his blood.

The same plan of salvation applies to all people, Jews and Gentiles alike. Everyone has sinned. All deserve to die. But Jesus came down to earth and died in our place. He became our substitute. God accepted his sacrifice as the payment for all the sins of every sinner in the world. Because sins have been paid for, God can now forgive the sinner. God sees the forgiven sinner as righteous. God declares the sinner justified. And it is all purely a free gift of God's grace.

Things to remember:

1. _____ has sinned and deserves to _____.

2. Christ _____ in our place to pay for our _____.

3. Because sins have been paid for, God can now _____ the sinner.

(Check your answers on page 54.)

(Read Romans 3:25b,26)

God did all of that to prove that he is fair. Because of his mercy he did not punish people for the sins they had committed before Jesus died for them. [26] God did that to prove in our own time that he is fair. He proved that he is right. He also made right with himself those who believe in Jesus.

Paul previously stated that God is fair in his dealings. Here is another example. Sinners deserve to die because sins are serious. God is not a kindly old grandfather who says to the sinner, "That's OK. I really wasn't all that serious about the Ten Commandments in the first place." No, sins need to be paid for. And they were paid for when Christ died on the cross with all our sins on his back. God's fairness assures us that our sins are paid for and we are forgiven.

(Read Romans 3:27,28)

[27] So who can brag? No one! Are people saved by obeying the law? Not at all! They are saved because of their faith. [28] We firmly believe that

Jesus dies on the cross to be punished for our sins.

people are made right with God because of their faith. They are not saved by obeying the law.

People are not saved by keeping the law. In fact, they are not saved by anything they do. Even believing is not a work that earns us anything. The Bible translation we are using says, "We are saved <u>because</u> we believe." This translation could be misunderstood to mean that by believing we have done something to earn salvation. It is more accurate to say, "We are saved <u>through</u> faith." Faith is merely the "hand" that receives forgiveness as a free gift from God. Recall that the subtitle of this book is *Righteous through Faith*.

<u>Things to remember:</u>

4. People are not saved by _____ they do.
5. Even _____ is not a work we do.
6. We are not saved _____ of faith but _____ faith.
7. Faith receives forgiveness as a _____ from God.

(Check your answers on page 54.)

(Read Romans 3:29-31)

[29] Is God the God of Jews only? Isn't he also the God of those who aren't Jews? Yes, he is their God too. [30] There is only one God. When those who are circumcised believe in him, he makes them right with himself. When those who are not circumcised believe in him, he also makes them right with himself. [31] Does faith make the law useless? Not at all! We agree with the law.

There is only one God. He is the God of both Jews and Gentiles. There is only one way of salvation and that is through faith in Jesus Christ. Trusting in him works for both Jews and Gentiles.

Righteous Through Faith (Romans 4:1-25)
Abraham's Faith

(Read Romans 4:1-5)

¹ What should we say about those things? What did our father Abraham discover about being right with God? ² Did he become right with God because of something he did? If so, he could brag about it. But he couldn't brag to God. ³ What do we find in Scripture? It says, "Abraham believed God. God accepted Abraham's faith, and so his faith made him right with God."—(*Genesis 15:6*)
⁴ When a man works, his pay is not considered a gift. It is owed to him. ⁵ But things are different with God. He makes evil people right with himself. If people trust in him, their faith is accepted even though they do not work. Their faith makes them right with God.

For both Jews and Gentiles God's plan of salvation is the same. It is by faith, not works. Paul starts out by giving us the example of Abraham, a Jew. Scripture says simply, "Abraham believed God." It says nothing about works. That is why great Abraham cannot boast. He did nothing. His faith received righteousness as a free gift from God.

In the everyday world, if a person works for someone, the money the boss gives him is earned. It is wages, not a gift. But with God it is totally different. God gives believers the righteousness Christ earned as a free gift.

Things to remember:
8. Both Jews and Gentiles are saved by _____ and not by _____.
9. Abraham did nothing to earn forgiveness; therefore he cannot _____.
(Check your answers on page 54.)

(Read Romans 4:6-8)

[6] King David says the same thing. He tells us how blessed some people are. God makes those people right with himself. But they don't have to do anything in return. David says,

[7] "Blessed are those
   whose lawless acts are forgiven.
Blessed are those
   whose sins are taken away.
[8] Blessed is the man
   whose sin the Lord never counts against him."—(*Psalm 32:1,2*)

King David is another example of a Jewish believer who trusted God's promise and was justified by that faith, without the addition of any works. King David's psalm shows us clearly that forgiveness of sins is the central feature of being justified by faith. That makes people right with God.

Paul has given an example of two circumcised Jewish believers, Abraham and David, being saved by faith. The apostle now moves on to show that the same plan of salvation works also for uncircumcised Gentiles who believe.

(Read Romans 4:9-12)

[9] Is that blessing only for those who are circumcised? Or is it also for those who are not circumcised? We have been saying that God accepted Abraham's faith, and so his faith made him right with God. [10] When did it happen? Was it after Abraham was circumcised, or before? It was before he was circumcised, not after! [11] He was circumcised as a sign of the covenant God had made with him. It showed that his faith had made him right with God before he was circumcised.
So Abraham is the father of all believers who have not been circumcised. God accepts their faith. So their faith makes them right with him. [12] Abraham is also the father of the circumcised who believe. So just being circumcised is not enough. Those who are circumcised must also follow the steps of our father Abraham. He had faith before he was circumcised.

David defeats Goliath with God's help.

Paul asks, "When did God count Abraham's faith as righteousness? Was it before he was circumcised or after?" The question is important because it determines whether uncircumcised Gentiles can be saved. To answer the question we need to look at the book of Genesis.

Genesis 12:1-3 tells us God asked Abraham at age 75 to leave his homeland and to move to a new country. There God would make him a great nation. Abraham believed God and went. He did not know at the time that he would have to wait 25 years for the birth of the promised son.

In Genesis 15:5,6 God repeated his promise, assuring Abraham that his descendants would be as many as the stars. Here we are told, "Abraham believed the Lord, and he credited it to him as righteousness." Abraham was right with God at this time.

Many years later, when Abraham was 99 years old, he still did not have the promised heir. God again repeated his promise of many descendants. This time he made a formal covenant with Abraham. That covenant required Abraham and his descendants to be circumcised (Genesis 17:9,10). The point is: Circumcision was introduced long after Abraham had already been declared righteous. Circumcision didn't make Abraham right with God. His faith did.

Things to remember:

10. When Paul talks of circumcised people he is referring to _____. Gentiles are called _____.
11. The question here is whether people can be right with God without doing anything, such as _____ _____.
12. Abraham was saved by faith, _____ he was circumcised and not after.
13. Only _____ saves; not anything we do.

(Check your answers on page 54.)

Circumcision obviously is not necessary for salvation. Only faith is. Therefore, believing Gentiles can also be saved. In this way, Abraham is the father of all believers, both the uncircumcised Gentile believers and also the circumcised Jewish believers.

(Read Romans 4:13-16)

[13] Abraham and his family received a promise. God promised that Abraham would receive the world. It would not come to him because he obeyed the law. It would come because of his faith, which made him right with God.
[14] Do those who obey the law receive the promise? If they do, faith would have no value. God's promise would be worthless. [15] The law brings God's anger. Where there is no law, the law can't be broken.
[16] The promise is based on God's grace. The promise comes by faith. All of Abraham's children will certainly receive the promise. And it is not only for those who are ruled by the law. Those who have the same faith that Abraham had are also included. He is the father of us all.

In this section Paul introduces a very important word. That word is "promise." There is also the contrasting word "law." A promise happens when someone says, "I will give you something. A law works in the other direction. It says,"Give me something" or "Do something for me."

God gave Abraham a very great promise—actually, a three-fold promise:

1) he would inherit the land he was going to;
2) he would have many descendants; and
3) from one family of those descendants, the Jewish nation, the promised Savior from sin would be born.

God did not ask for something from Abraham. God promised to give him something.

Paul says in verse 16, "The promise is based on God's grace. The promise comes by faith." Grace is a term that speaks of God's love in action. It is the love that makes him want to give us something. As such, it is closely related to "promise." A promise depends totally on the generosity of the one making the promise. The promise goes unfulfilled if the recipient does not trust the giver. A promise requires faith. God promised; Abraham believed, and it was counted to him as righteousness.

Things to remember:

14. God made a three-fold promise to Abraham. He promised him:

   a)_____,

   b)_____ _____, and

   c) _____.

15. To be fulfilled, a promise requires _____ on the part of the person receiving the promise.

16. Abraham _____ God's promise.

17. There was no _____ requiring that Abraham do something to get the promise fulfilled.

(Check your answers on page 54.)

(Read Romans 4:17-22)

[17] It is written, "I have made you a father of many nations."—(*Genesis 17:5*) God considers Abraham to be our father. The God that Abraham believed in gives life to the dead. Abraham's God also speaks of things that do not exist as if they do exist.

[18] When there was no reason for hope, Abraham believed because he had hope. He became the father of many nations, exactly as God had promised. God said, "That is how many children you will have."—(*Genesis 15:5*)

[19] Without becoming weak in his faith, Abraham accepted the fact that he was past the time when he could have children. At that time he was about 100 years old. He also realized that Sarah was too old to have children.

[20] But he kept believing in God's promise. He became strong in his faith. He gave glory to God. [21] He was absolutely sure that God had the power to do what he had promised. [22] That's why "God accepted Abraham because he believed. So his faith made him right with God."

God had promised Abraham that he would have many descendants. But he had to wait many years before receiving any children. During all this time Abraham continued to trust God's promise. Paul says that Abraham believed in a God who "gives life to the dead." In Abraham's case that is clearly what God did.

When Abraham and his wife Sarah were both "dead" as far as child-bearing was concerned, God repeated his promise of many descendants. God assured the 99 year-old Abraham and his 90 year-old wife that within a year they would have a son. God's promise was fulfilled in the birth of their son Isaac. Abraham believed God's three-fold promise and it was credited to him as righteousness.

Things to remember:

18. Abraham and Sarah had to wait _____ years for a son.
19. Abraham and Sarah could be considered _____ as far as child-bearing was concerned. Even so, Abraham continued to _____ God's promises.

(Check your answers on page 54.)

(Read Romans 4:23-25)

[23] The words "God accepted Abraham's faith" were written not only for Abraham. [24] They were written also for us. We believe in the God who raised Jesus our Lord from the dead. So God will accept our faith and make us right with himself.
[25] Jesus was handed over to die for our sins. He was raised to life in order to make us right with God.

The Bible's account of Abraham being saved by faith was not written just for Abraham. It is also for us. Salvation by faith in God's promises is still the only way to be saved, and it is available also for us.

An angel at Jesus' grave tells the women that Jesus is risen.

God's three-fold promise to Abraham included the promise of many descendants. Included among those descendants was the promised Savior, Jesus of Nazareth. He came down to earth to be our substitute. He lived a perfect life for us and he was handed over to die for our sins. As proof that his death paid for all our sins, God the Father, who gives life to the dead, raised him to life again on Easter morning. He now invites us to trust in him for life and salvation. By faith in Christ we also, like Abraham, are forgiven and justified. In this way we become descendants of Abraham, the father of all believers.

Things to remember:

20. The Bible tells of Abraham being saved through faith for _____ benefit. We too will be saved through _____ such as Abraham had.

21. Jesus lived a perfect _____ for us and died an innocent _____ for us.

22. God the Father _____ Jesus from death to prove that he was satisfied with Jesus' sacrifice for the world's sin.

(Check your answers on page 54.)

The Believer's Peace and Joy (Romans 5:1-11)

(Read Romans 5:1,2)

[1] We have been made right with God because of our faith. Now we have peace with him because of our Lord Jesus Christ. [2] Through faith in Jesus we have received God's grace. In that grace we stand. We are full of joy because we expect to share in God's glory.

A holy God cannot tolerate sin. If he did, he would no longer be holy. There has to be enmity between a holy God and sinful people. However, through Jesus' perfect life and innocent death he has paid for our sins. They are gone. God does not hold them against us any longer. The enmity between God and the sinner is gone. Now there is peace.

In speaking of this change Paul writes, "Through faith in Jesus we have received God's grace." <u>Grace</u> is again the word that shows us God's eager desire to give. We could say here, "Through faith in Jesus we have received God's <u>gift</u>." Forgiveness has been earned by Jesus, not by us. It is a free gift from God. With our sins forgiven we are at peace with God. When there is peace with God, there is also the joy of knowing that we will spend eternity with God in heaven.

<u>Things to remember:</u>

23. Forgiveness of sins is a _____ from God.

24. With our sins forgiven we have _____ with God.

25. When there is peace with God, there is also _____.

26. This joy looks forward to spending eternity with _____ in _____.

(Check your answers on page 54.)

(Read Romans 5:3-5)

[3] And that's not all. We are full of joy even when we suffer. We know that our suffering gives us the strength to go on. [4] The strength to go on produces character. Character produces hope. [5] And hope will never let us down. God has poured his love into our hearts. He did it through the Holy Spirit, whom he has given to us.

There is great joy in looking forward to an eternity in heaven. But our joy is not limited to the future. There is joy also here and now. Suffering and hardship will come into our lives, but even these are good. They strengthen our faith and give us greater hope. "Faith" and "hope" are closely related terms, almost interchangeable.

Paul has indicated a number of times that faith is necessary for the sinner to become right with God. But he has not told us how the sinner gets this faith or hope. Now he adds that detail. "God has poured his love into our hearts. He did it through the Holy Spirit, whom he has given to us."

Note that we neither can nor need to do anything to get the Spirit. He comes to us as a gift from God the Father. The Spirit teaches us how God has poured his love into our hearts.

Things to remember:

27. Suffering and hardship strengthen our _____.
28. The _____ _____ teaches us how God has poured out his love into our hearts. We do not need to do anything to get the Holy Spirit. The Father _____ him to us.

(Check your answers on page 54.)

(Read Romans 5:6-8)

[6] At just the right time Christ died for ungodly people. He died for us when we had no power of our own. [7] It is unusual for anyone to die for a godly person. Maybe someone would be willing to die for a good person. [8] But here is how God has shown his love for us. While we were still sinners, Christ died for us.

Rarely will one person volunteer to die for another. When it does happen, he almost certainly agrees to die for a good person, not a bad one. But look what God did for us. When we were sinners, ungodly people, enemies of God, Christ died for us. God loved us that much! And it is this love of God that the Holy Spirit now pours into our hearts. He teaches us to love God and to believe in him. In this way the Holy Spirit creates faith in people's hearts.

Things to remember:

29. We know God loves us because Christ _____ for us.
30. Christ died for us when we were _____.
31. God has poured his love into our hearts. He did it through the _____ _____ whom he has given to us.
32. The Holy Spirit works _____ in our hearts.

(Check your answers on page 54.)

(Read Romans 5:9-11)

[9] The blood of Christ has made us right with God. So we are even more sure that Jesus will save us from God's anger. [10] Once we were God's enemies. But we have been brought back to him because his Son has died for us. Now that God has brought us back, we are even more secure. We know that we will be saved because Christ lives. [11] And that is not all. We are full of joy in God because of our Lord Jesus Christ. Because of him, God has brought us back to himself.

Things to remember:

33. When we were _____ of God _____ died to make us friends of God.
34. We know that we will be saved because _____ lives.
35. Because we know we will be saved, we are full of _____.

(Check your answers on page 54.)

Death through Adam, Life through Christ (Romans 5:12-20)

(Read Romans 5:12-14)

[12] Sin entered the world because one man sinned. And death came because of sin. Everyone sinned, so death came to all people.
[13] Before the law was given, sin was in the world. But sin is not judged

when there is no law. [14] Death ruled from the time of Adam to the time of Moses. Death ruled even over those who did not sin as Adam did. He broke God's command. But he also became a pattern of the One who was going to come.

Adam and Eve sinned in the Garden of Eden when they ate of the forbidden fruit. Sin causes death. Adam's sin brought death to the world. All people die because all people are sinners. It is important to realize that sin is not only bad things people do, but it is also a condition. Sinfulness is something we inherit from our sinful parents. The psalmist says, "I know I've been a sinner ever since I was born. I've been a sinner ever since my mother became pregnant with me" (Psalm 51:5).

What Adam did had an effect on all people. In this way there is a parallel between Adam and the "One who was going to come," namely Jesus. In both cases, what they did had an effect on the whole world.

Things to remember:

36. Adam's sin brought sin and _____ into the world.
37. All people are sinful because they _____ sin from their parents.
38. Adam and Christ are alike in that what they did affected the _____ _____.

(Check your answers on page 54.)

(Read Romans 5:15,16)

[15] God's gift is different from Adam's sin. Many people died because of the sin of that one man. But it was even more sure that God's grace would also come through one man. That man is Jesus Christ. God's gift of grace was more than enough for the whole world.

[16] The result of God's gift is different from the result of Adam's sin. God judged one sin. That brought guilt. But after many sins, God's gift made people right with him.

In one way what Adam and Christ did was similar. What each did affected the whole world. But what Jesus Christ did was also far different. What Adam did brought death for all. What Christ did brought a precious gift for all. That gift is forgiveness of sins and the righteousness that makes us acceptable to God.

(Read Romans 5:17-19)

[17] One man sinned, and death ruled because of his sin. But we are even more sure of what will happen because of what the one man, Jesus Christ, has done. Those who receive the rich supply of God's grace will rule with Christ in his kingdom. They have received God's gift and have been made right with him.
[18] One man's sin brought guilt to all people. So also one right act made all people right with God. And all who are right with God will live. [19] Many people were made sinners because one man did not obey. But one man did obey. That is why many people will be made right with God.

What Adam did brought death into the world. What Christ did brought life. His perfect life and innocent death earned the righteousness that makes sinners right with God. This righteousness is there for every sinner. Paul calls it a "rich supply of God's grace."

But we need to read Paul's whole sentence carefully. He says, "Those who receive the rich supply of God's grace will rule with Christ in his kingdom." By God's grace Christ's righteousness is there for every sinner in the world. But some people are too proud to accept that righteousness as a gift (by grace). They don't want to admit that they can do nothing to get right with God. They think they can do something to earn righteousness with God. Lacking faith and trust in what Christ has done for them, they are unbelievers. Such people do not receive God's gracious gift of salvation, even though it is there for them.

Things to remember:

39. Christ's sacrifice earned righteousness for

_____.

40. Some people don't believe that. They think they can

_____ righteousness by what they do.

41. Such people will not receive God's gift of

_____.

(Check your answers on page 54.)

(Read Romans 5:20,21)

[20] The law was given so that sin would increase. But where sin increased, God's grace increased even more. [21] Sin ruled because of death. So also grace rules in the lives of those who are right with God. The grace of God brings eternal life because of what Jesus Christ our Lord has done.

God's law shows us our sin and condemns us to death. But God's grace ("gift") is stronger than the law. God's grace gives us credit for what Christ did for us. The gift of his righteousness saves us. Formerly sin ruled us. Now God's grace rules us. We will want to show that change in our lives. In the next three chapters Paul speaks of how God's grace changes a Christian's life and actions.

Things to remember-Answers

1. Everyone, die; 2. died, sins; 3. forgive; 4. anything; 5. believing; 6. because, through; 7. gift; 8. faith, works; 9. boast; 10. Jews, uncircumcised; 11. being circumcised; 12. before; 13. faith; 14. a) land, b) many descendents, c) a Savior from sin; 15. faith/trust; 16. believed; 17. law; 18. many; 19. dead, trust; 20. our, faith; 21. life, death; 22. raised; 23. gift; 24. peace; 25. joy; 26. God, heaven; 27. faith; 28. Holy Spirit, gives; 29. died; 30. sinners; 31. Holy Spirit; 32. faith; 33. enemies, Christ; 34. Jesus; 35. joy; 36. death; 37. inherit; 38. whole world; 39, everyone; 40. earn; 41. salvation.

TEST - Righteous Through Faith: A Study of the Epistle to the Romans

Section 3

Please review the "Things to remember."

1. _____ has sinned and deserves to _____.

2. Christ _____ in our place to pay for our _____. Because our sins have been paid for, God can now _____ us.

3. People are not saved by _____ they do. Even _____ is not a work we do.

4. We are not saved because of faith but _____ faith.

5. Abraham was saved through faith _____ he was circumcised and not after. Only _____ saves; not anything we do.

6. God made a three-fold promise to Abraham. He promised him:
   a)_____ ,
   b)_____ , and
   c)_____ .

7. To be fulfilled, a promise requires _____ on the part of the person receiving the promise.

.

8. Abraham and Sarah could be considered _____ as far as child-bearing was concerned. Even so, Abraham continued to _____ God's promises.

9. The Bible tells of Abraham being saved through faith for _____ benefit. We too will be saved through _____ such as Abraham had.

.

10. God the Father _____ Jesus from death to prove that he was satisfied with Jesus' sacrifice for the world's sin.

11. With our sins forgiven we have _____ with God. When there is peace with God, there is also _____. This joy looks forward to spending eternity with _____ in _____.

12. Suffering and hardship strengthen our _____.

13. The _____ _____ teaches us how God has poured out his love into our hearts. We do not need to do anything to get the Holy Spirit. The Father _____ him to us.

14. When we were _____ of God _____ died to make us friends of God.

15. Adam's sin brought sin and _____ into the world. All people are sinful because they have _____ sin from their parents.

16. Christ's sacrifice earned righteousness for _____. Some people don't believe that. They think they can _____ righteousness by what they do. Such people will not receive God's gift of _____.

(Check your answers on page 192.)

RIGHTEOUS
THROUGH FAITH

SECTION 4:
New Life in Christ

Romans 6:1 – 8:39

Righteous Through Faith:
A Study of the Epistle to the Romans

SECTION FOUR:
New Life in Christ (Romans 6:1-8:39)

Free From Sin (Romans 6:1-14)

(Read Romans 6:1-8)

[1] What should we say then? Should we keep on sinning so that God's grace can increase? [2] Not at all! As far as sin is concerned, we are dead. So how can we keep on sinning? [3] All of us were baptized into Christ Jesus. Don't you know that we were baptized into his death? [4] By being baptized, we were buried <u>with</u> Christ into his death. Christ has been raised from the dead by the Father's glory. And like Christ we also can live a new life.

[5] By being baptized, we have been joined <u>with</u> him in his death. We will certainly also be joined <u>with</u> him in his resurrection. [6] We know that what we used to be was nailed to the cross <u>with</u> him. That happened so our sinful bodies would lose their power. We are no longer slaves of sin. [7] Those who have died have been set free from sin.

[8] We died <u>with</u> Christ. So we believe that we will also live <u>with</u> him.

The Bible tells us that all people are born sinful. And in their lives sinful people add many sins by the bad things they do every day. For those sins God should punish the sinner with eternal death. But in his love God sent his Son, Jesus Christ, to be the sinner's substitute.

On the cross God punished Jesus instead of us. Our sins are now forgiven. When we see what price Jesus had to pay for our forgiveness and how much our loving God hates sin, are we going to keep on sinning? Paul answers emphatically, "Not at all!"

By ourselves we could never withstand the urge to sin. But a gracious God has given us a powerful source of help. He has joined us to Christ by the gift of baptism. Read the verses 4-8 once more and notice that six times Paul uses the word "with." By our baptism we have been joined <u>with</u> Christ.

Baptism is a "sacrament," that is, a sacred act God has commanded. Through it he promises to bless us. To an earthly element (water in the case of baptism) God attaches a promise. Through baptism the Holy Spirit works faith in the baptized person and forgives his sin. That makes the baptized person a child of God. It joins him to Christ. Through baptism the believer has died with Christ. He has been buried with Christ. He has also been raised to a new life with Christ. Paul says, "Those who have died have been set free from sin. We died with Christ. So we believe that we will also live with him."

Things to remember:

1. Through baptism the Holy Spirit works _____ in the baptized person's heart.
2. Baptism joins us with _____.
3. Joined to Christ in baptism, we are now _____ to sin.
4. Through baptism we have been raised to a _____ _____ with Christ.

(Check your answers on page 90.)

(Read Romans 6:9-14a)

[9] We know that Christ was raised from the dead and will never die again. Death doesn't control him anymore. [10] When he died, he died once and for all time as far as sin is concerned. Now that he lives, he lives as far as God is concerned.

[11] In the same way, consider yourselves to be dead as far as sin is concerned. Now that you believe in Christ Jesus, consider yourselves to be alive as far as God is concerned.

[12] So don't let sin rule your body, which is going to die. Don't obey its evil longings. [13] Don't give the parts of your body to serve sin. Don't let them be used to do evil. Instead, give yourselves to God. You have been

Philip baptizes the Eunuch of Ethiopia.

brought from death to life. Give the parts of your body to him to do what is right.

[14] Sin will not be your master.

Christ not only died <u>for</u> sin but Paul says he also died <u>to</u> sin. To be dead to sin means that sin has no power over a person. As far as sin is concerned Jesus died to sin. It has no control over him. As far as his life is concerned, he now lives to God. What God wants controls Jesus.

In baptism we were connected to Christ's death and also to his life. Paul now draws a parallel: "In the same way consider yourselves to be dead as far as sin is concerned. Now that you believe in Christ Jesus, consider yourselves to be alive as far as God is concerned."

We know what pain and sorrow our sins cost Jesus. They cost him his life. We will not want to repeat those sins. So do not let sin rule in your body. The apostle gives some general warnings. First he warns against bad thoughts. "Don't obey [sin's] evil longings." Then he warns against bad actions. "Don't give the parts of your body to serve sin."

There are many bad things people do. A child of God will try to avoid doing bad things. But the new life of the baptized child of God doesn't only try to avoid doing evil. It also wants to do what pleases God.

Things to remember:

5. Christ not only died _____ sin but he also died _____ sin.
6. Sin has no control over a _____ person.
7. With Christ we died to _____ in our baptism. We will now try to avoid doing _____ _____ and we will try to do what _____ God.

(Check your answers on page 90.)

Free From Law (Romans 6:14-7:6)

(Read Romans 6:14b-18)

Law does not rule you. God's grace has set you free. [15] What should we say then? Should we sin because we are not ruled by law but by God's grace? Not at all!
[16] Don't you know that when you give yourselves to obey someone you become that person's slave? You can be slaves of sin. Then you will die. Or you can be slaves who obey God. Then you will live a godly life. [17] You used to be slaves of sin. But thank God that with your whole heart you obeyed the teachings you were given! [18] You have been set free from sin. You have become slaves to right living.

God is a just and holy God. He has every right to make laws for his creatures. He rightly expects people to do what he asks of them. If people could do what pleases God they would be acceptable to God on their own merits. But all people are sinners. They do not do what pleases God. They cannot get right with God by what they do. They cannot be saved by keeping God's law.

The only way for people to get right with God is for God to give them righteousness as a gift. And that is what God has done. God the Father sent his Son Jesus into the world. The Son lived a perfect life to earn righteousness for us. He died an innocent death on the cross to earn forgiveness of sins for us. And now God gives us those blessings "by grace" as a gift.

In appreciation for God's great gift, God's grace, the forgiven sinner will now fight against sin. He will want to live a new life and do what pleases God. He will do so because he is "ruled" by grace.

Paul tells the Romans that they are now "free" to do what God asks of them. That was not always the case. Previously under the law they could not please God. Rather, they earned God's anger by breaking his commands. "You used to be slaves of sin," the apostle writes, "but thank God that with

Moses smashes the Ten Commandments.

your whole heart you obeyed the teaching you were given."

The verses we are currently discussing started with the statement, "Law does not rule you. God's grace has set you free." How did that great change take place? We have already heard an answer earlier when the author reminded his readers that through their baptism they had been joined with Christ. Now he gives a further answer. Just as the Holy Spirit uses baptism to bring people to faith, in the same way, he uses the Bible's message of the gospel. Paul reminds the Romans, "Thank God that with your whole heart you obeyed the teaching you were given."

Remember that Paul has not yet been to Rome, but somewhere his readers have heard the message of the gospel brought to them by Christian preachers or teachers. The Romans heard the message of God's love and they believed it. The Word worked faith in their hearts. As forgiven sinners, made right with God, they now want to serve him in their new life of faith.

Things to remember:

8. People cannot keep God's _____.
    That's why they cannot be _____ by it.
9. Believers receive Christ's righteousness "by grace."
    That means it is a _____.
10. Out of thankfulness for this gift, believers will want to
    _____.
11. Living a new life is a fruit of faith. We previously heard
    that the Holy Spirit creates faith through the sacrament
    of _____. Now Paul adds that the Spirit also
    works through the _____.

(Check your answers on page 90.)

An Illustration From Slavery

Slavery was very common at the time Paul wrote to the Romans. Many people who were defeated in battle were

Mary listens to God's Word.

carried off as prisoners of war. In this way they lost their freedom. They were sold into slavery and came to be owned by masters. A slave could not make his own decisions. He was ruled by his master.

Paul is asking his readers to look at their lives and see who is in control. Does sin control them, or their new life in Christ?

(Read Romans 6:19-23)

Because you are human, you find this hard to understand. So I have said it in a way that will help you understand it. You used to give the parts of your body to be slaves to unclean living. You were becoming more and more evil. Now give your bodies to be slaves to right living. Then you will become holy.
[20] Once you were slaves of sin. At that time right living did not control you. [21] What benefit did you gain from doing the things you are now ashamed of? Those things lead to death!
[22] You have been set free from sin. God has made you his slaves. The benefit you gain leads to holy living. And the end result is eternal life. [23] When you sin, the pay you get is death. But God gives you the gift of eternal life because of what Christ Jesus our Lord has done.

Paul closed the previous paragraph with the statement, "You used to be slaves of sin. But thank God that with your whole heart you obeyed the teachings you were given! You have been set free from sin. You have become slaves to right living."

Paul uses the picture of slavery to illustrate the situation of a person who is under the control of a master. All people are conceived and born as sinners. They are under the control of sin. That was the case also with the Romans. "Once you were slaves of sin. At that time right living did not control you." That was a bad situation, because it could only lead to death.

But the good news is: "You have been set free from sin" (v 22). It is all God's doing. Jesus died to pay for our sins.

The Holy Spirit gives us the faith to believe that God the Father has accepted Jesus' payment in our place. In this way God has redeemed us (bought us back). He now owns us. Paul can say we are God's slaves because God guides and directs us.

Such guidance and direction from God is not a burden. Living a holy life is what believers want to do to thank God. Furthermore, it brings blessed results. Being under the control of sin leads to death. Being God's slaves "leads to holy living. And the end result is eternal life." Once more the apostle reminds us that eternal life is a gift made possible "because of what Christ Jesus our Lord has done."

Things to remember:

12. A slave is under the control of his _____.
13. All people are born sinners. Therefore they are under the control of _____.
14. Christ freed us from the control of sin by

_____.
15. Freed from the control of sin, we now want to lead a _____ life in order to _____ God.

(Check your answers on page 90.)

An Illustration From Marriage Laws

The apostle Paul is a good teacher. He uses well-known things to explain what is not so well-known. In the previous section he explained what it means for someone to be under the control of another. In a way it is like being a slave. A person can be under the control of sin and lead a bad life or under the control of Christ and lead a new life. Clearly we do not want to be under the control of sin.

In these next verses Paul introduces something else that can control people. That is what he calls "the law." These are the things a holy God rightly expects of people. We could call them the Ten Commandments. What kind of control do they have over us? Paul explains that with another illustration. This time he uses the marriage laws that his readers are sure to know.

(Read Romans 7:1-3)

¹ Brothers and sisters, I am speaking to you who know the law. Don't you know that the law has authority over us only as long as we are alive? ² For example, by law a married woman is joined to her husband as long as he is living. But suppose her husband dies. Then the marriage law no longer applies to her. ³ But suppose that married woman gets married again while her husband is still alive. Then she is called a woman who commits adultery. But suppose her husband dies. Then she is free from that law. She is not guilty of adultery even if she marries another man.

In these verses Paul is stating what he expects his readers to know. Marriage rules control <u>living</u> people. The marriage rules no longer apply if one or the other spouse dies. For example, if a married woman marries another man while her husband is still living, the marriage law condemns her as guilty of adultery. But if her husband has died, she is free of the law. As a widow she is free to marry again. The main point for us to note is that death changes things. Death frees people from the control of law.

Things to remember:
16. Marriage rules control _____ people.
17. Marriage rules no longer apply if one of the spouses

_____ _____.

(Check your answers on page 90.)

(Read Romans 7:4-6)

⁴ My brothers and sisters, when Christ died you also died as far as the law is concerned. Then it became possible for you to belong to him. He was raised from the dead. Now our lives can be useful to God. ⁵ Our sinful

nature used to control us. The law stirred up sinful longings in our bodies. So the things we did resulted in death.

[6] But now we have died to what used to control us. We have been set free from the law. Now we serve in the new way of the Holy Spirit. We no longer serve in the old way of the written law.

Death frees people from the control of law. In verse four Paul applies that truth to God's plan of salvation. He says, "When Christ died you also died as far as the law is concerned." Christ Jesus, the holy Son of God, came down from heaven to lead the perfect life that God's law demanded. After Christ's perfect keeping of the law, it could make no more demands of him. It had no more control over him. Jesus could be said to be dead to the law.

Paul previously told us that through baptism we are united with Christ in his death. With him we too are dead to the law. We are no longer "married" to the law. A new union is now possible. We are now free to belong to Christ. In fact, Scripture often talks of believers, the church, as being the "bride" of Christ.

Under the control of the law our sinful nature used to do bad things. The demands of the law irritate people and they rebel. That is why Paul can say "The law stirred up sinful longings in our bodies."

But dying with Christ changed that. The apostle writes: "But now we have died to what used to control us. We have been set free from the law. Now we serve in the new way of the Holy Spirit. We no longer serve in the old way of the written law."

"The old way of the law" made demands of us. It said, "You have to do this and that. Then you will be right with God." The new way of the Spirit says, "Christ has done everything for you. God's gives you his righteousness as a free gift." Salvation is by grace, not by works of the law.

Things to remember:

18. Death frees people from the control of the _____.
19. Christ died to the _____.
20. Through our baptism we have _____ with Christ.
21 With Christ, we too are free from the control of the _____.
22. We are now free to serve God in the new way of the _____.

(Check your answers on page 90.)

The Useful Purpose of the Law

(Read Romans 7:7-13)

[7] What should we say then? That the law is sin? Not at all! I wouldn't have known what sin was unless the law had told me. The law said, "Do not want what belongs to other people."—(*Exodus 20:17; Deuteronomy 5:21*) If the law hadn't said that, I would not have known what it was like to want what belonged to others. [8] But the commandment gave sin an opportunity. Sin caused me to want all kinds of things that belonged to others. No one can break a law that doesn't exist.

[9] Before I knew about the law, I was alive. But then the commandment came. Sin came to life, and I died. [10] I found that the commandment that was supposed to bring life actually brought death. [11] When the commandment gave sin the opportunity, sin tricked me. It used the commandment to put me to death. [12] So the law is holy. The commandment also is holy and right and good.

[13] Did what is good cause me to die? Not at all! Sin had to be recognized for what it really is. So it produced death in me through what was good. Because of the commandment, sin became totally sinful.

Paul said a number of times that it is good for the believer to be free from the control of law. But does that mean the law itself is bad. Paul says, "Not at all!" When Paul uses the term "law" here we can think of the Ten Commandments. He refers to the 9th and 10th Commandments when he quotes from Exodus 20:17, which forbids "coveting" (wanting other

King Ahab covets Naboth's vineyard.

people's property).

Paul admits that he would not have known coveting was wrong if the commandment had not told him so. In verse nine he says, "Before I knew about the law, I was alive. But then the commandment came. Sin came to life, and I died." At first Paul did not realize he was in trouble with God. He thought he was "alive." But then he found out about the commandment forbidding coveting. Now he knew coveting was wrong, but he still wanted the things belonging to his neighbor. That was a sin. Sin made him worthy of death before a just and holy God.

Paul uses the 9th and 10th Commandments as an example, but he could have used any of the commandments. All of the Ten Commandments are good. They protect valuable things. The Fifth Commandment protects human life. The Sixth Commandment protects marriage. The Seventh Commandment protects people's property. God's Commandments (the "law") are good. But that leads to Paul's question, "Did what is good cause me to die?" And he answers, "Not at all!"

What useful purpose did the law serve? He says, "Sin had to be recognized for what it really is." God's law tells people what God expects of them. When they do not do what God's commandments require, then they realize their actions are wrong. They are sinning and deserve to die.

By comparing his behavior to what God expected of him, Paul could see just how bad he was. Through the law sin became "totally sinful." It showed him that he could not save himself by keeping the law. Rather, the law showed him his sin and his need for a savior from sin.

Things to remember:

23. The law shows us what _____ expects of people.

24. Not doing what God expects is a _____ for which the sinner should _____.

25. The law is good because it shows us our _____ and our need for a _____ from sin.

(Check your answers on page 90.)

Struggling With Sin

(Read Romans 7:14-20)

[14] We know that the law is holy. But I am not. I have been sold to be a slave of sin. [15] I don't understand what I do. I don't do what I want to do. Instead, I do what I hate to do. [16] I do what I don't want to do. So I agree that the law is good. [17] As it is, I am no longer the one who does these things. It is sin living in me that does them.

[18] I know there is nothing good in my sinful nature. I want to do what is good, but I can't. [19] I don't do the good things I want to do. I keep on doing the evil things I don't want to do. [20] I do what I don't want to do. But I am not really the one who is doing it. It is sin living in me.

The commandments tell us what God expects. These commandments are good and holy. But people are not holy. They disobey the commandments. Like Paul they are slaves of sin. They have to say with the apostle, "I know there is nothing good in my sinful nature. I want to do what is good, but I can't." And with them we too have to admit, "I don't do the good things I want to do. I keep on doing the evil things I don't want to do."

Why is this struggle with sin going on? Because the believer, who by faith in Christ is a child of God, still has a sinful nature. Every day this sinful nature tries to get control.

Things to remember:

26. A believing child of God wants to do what is

_____.

73

27. A believing child of God still has a _____ nature.

28. This sinful nature always tries to _____

_____.

(Check your answers on page 90.)

(Read Romans 7:21-25)

[21] Here is the <u>law</u> I find working in me. When I want to do good, evil is right there with me. [22] Deep inside me I find joy in God's <u>law</u>. [23] But I see another <u>law</u> working in the parts of my body. It fights against the <u>law</u> of my mind. It makes me a prisoner of the <u>law</u> of sin. That <u>law</u> controls the parts of my body.

[24] What a terrible failure I am! Who will save me from this sin that brings death to my body? [25] I give thanks to God. He will do it through Jesus Christ our Lord.

So in my mind I am a slave to God's law. But in my sinful nature I am a slave to the law of sin.

Go back and read verses 21-23 once more. Notice the underlined words. Six (6) times Paul uses the word "law." The trouble is that "law" does not always mean the same thing. Let's substitute a word in each case that explains what is meant and makes the meaning clearer.

[21] Here is the (pattern) I find working in me. When I want to do good, evil is right there with me. [22] Deep inside me I find joy in God's (commandments). [23] But I see another (force) working in the parts of my body. It fights against the (controlling force) of my mind. It makes me a prisoner of the (control) of sin. That (force) controls the parts of my body.

Paul is here speaking of what is often called a believer's "old Adam" and his "new man." From Adam, who fell into sin, all people have inherited a sinful nature. This evil nature, this old Adam, rebels against God and breaks God's commandments every day.

74

Jesus suffers and dies to pay for our sins.
He is mocked by soldiers.

When through the gospel the Holy Spirit works faith in a sinner's heart, then the believer becomes a different person. He now has a "new man." Out of thankfulness this new man wants to do what God wants. Deep inside he finds joy in God's commandments.

But there is a problem. There is a pattern in Paul's life that he doesn't like at all! Whenever Paul's new man wants to do what's good, another force shows up. That is the old Adam. This old Adam tries to keep the new man in the believer from doing good. A struggle for control always follows.

In the life of every believer there is a constant battle going on. And the new man does not always win. We see that in our own life. The good we want to do, we don't do. The evil we don't want to do, that we keep right on doing. It leads us also to say with Paul, "What a terrible failure I am!" And with Paul it leads us to ask, "Who will save me from this sin that brings death to my body?"

If we had to keep the law to be saved, it would be hopeless. We could never be righteous before God. But thank God we do not have to earn righteousness by ourselves. Christ has done that for us by his perfect life. And by his innocent death he has paid for what we so often do wrong. And the good news is: Christ gives us his righteousness as a gift. Covered by his righteousness, we look perfectly holy to God.

Things to remember:

29. Coming to faith gives the believer a _____ _____.

30. This new man wants to do _____ _____.

31. Every believer still has a _____ nature.

32. This sinful nature is often called our _____
_____.

33. The old Adam always wants to do _____
_____.

34. Every day the "new man" and the old Adam
_____ with each other.

35. When our old Adam leads us to sin, we need to trust in
_____ for the righteousness that makes
us look holy before God.

(Check your answers on page 90.)

The Holy Spirit Controls Christians' Lives (Romans 8:1-17)

(Read Romans 8:1-2)

[1] Those who belong to Christ Jesus are no longer under God's sentence. [2] I am now controlled by the law of the Holy Spirit. That law gives me life because of what Christ Jesus has done. It has set me free from the law of sin that brings death.

The most important word in this whole section (Romans 8:1-17) is the word "control." If you substitute the word "control" for "law" the meaning of verse 2 becomes clear. [2] I am now controlled by the (control) of the Holy Spirit. That (control) gives me life because of what Christ Jesus has done. It has set me free from the (control) of sin that brings death.

We have already heard that the believer has two forces at work in him. One is the sinful nature we were born with, our "old Adam." It wants to lead us into sin. The other force is our "new man," created in us by the Holy Spirit when he brought us to faith. The new man wants to do what pleases God. Both forces are active in the believer. In fact, they fight with each other, but it is the new man, guided by the Holy Spirit, who is in control of the child of God.

77

(Read Romans 8:3,4)

[3] The written law was made weak by our sinful nature. But God did what the written law could not do. He made his Son to be like those who have a sinful nature. He sent him to be an offering for sin. In that way, he judged sin in his Son's human body. [4] Now we can do everything the law requires. Our sinful nature no longer controls the way we live. The Holy Spirit now controls the way we live.

Here the word "law" has its more common meaning of "commandment." The "written law" refers to the Ten Commandments engraved on stone tablets on Mount Sinai. These commandments make demands that sinful people cannot keep. That is why the law is called "weak." It cannot save people because they cannot keep the commandments a holy God demands.

What the law could not do, God himself did for us. He sent his Son to be born of a human mother. Jesus Christ, true God, became also true man. In this way he could be the offering that was needed to pay for the sins of the world.

God "judged sin in his Son's human body." With sin paid for by Christ's death, there is now forgiveness for every sin ever committed. The Holy Spirit brings people to faith. Through this faith they accept the forgiveness Christ has earned for them. Where there is forgiveness of sin there is peace with God and the sure hope of eternal life in heaven.

Out of appreciation for such priceless gifts, believers now want to thank God. They want to keep God's commandments. They do not do it to earn salvation. That has been taken care of by Christ. They do it in order to thank and praise God. Now they are under the control of the Spirit, not their sinful nature.

Things to remember:
36. The commandments make demands that a sinner cannot

_____.

Jesus is born.

37. A sinner cannot be saved by keeping the
    _____. That is why Paul says the
    law is _____.

38. God sent his Son to be born as a human so he could be
    an _____ for sin.

39. Christ's death earned _____ for the sins
    of the whole world.

40. A forgiven sinner is under the control of the
    _____.

41. A forgiven sinner wants to _____God.

(Check your answers on page 90.)

(Read Romans 8:5-8)

Note the word "control" repeated four (4) times.

[5] Don't live under the <u>control</u> of your sinful nature. If you do, you will think about what your sinful nature wants. Live under the <u>control</u> of the Holy Spirit. If you do, you will think about what the Spirit wants.
[6] The way a sinful person thinks leads to death. But the mind <u>controlled</u> by the Spirit brings life and peace. [7] The sinful mind is at war with God. It does not obey God's law. It can't. [8] Those who are <u>controlled</u> by their sinful nature can't please God.

    The Holy Spirit brings people to faith and gives them a "new man." This new man is able to make proper choices. Paul urges his readers to make the right choice. He says, "Don't live under the control of your sinful nature." Doing so brings bad results. "The way a sinful person thinks leads to death."

    Rather, Paul urges his readers, "Live under the control of the Holy Spirit." That brings great blessings. "The mind controlled by the Spirit brings life and peace."

    How does this life and peace come to us? Paul says it comes through the Holy Spirit who lives in us.

(Read Romans 8:9-11)

[9] But your sinful nature does not control you. The Holy Spirit controls you. The Spirit of God lives in you. Anyone who does not have the Spirit of Christ does not belong to Christ.

[10] Christ lives in you. So your body is dead because of sin. But your spirit is alive because you have been made right with God. [11] The Spirit of the One who raised Jesus from the dead is living in you. So the God who raised Christ from the dead will also give life to your bodies, which are going to die. He will do this by the power of his Spirit, who lives in you.

These verses introduce us to a very great mystery. In many places the Bible teaches us that there are three persons (Father, Son, and Holy Spirit) in one God. The God of the Bible is a "triune" (three in one) God. We cannot explain that mathematically, but in faith we believe it because God's Word teaches it.

The apostle Paul in verse 11 refers to the three separate persons when he writes, "The <u>Spirit</u> of the <u>One</u> who raised <u>Jesus</u> from the dead is living in you." The Spirit works in perfect harmony with the Father and the Son. This Spirit lives in the believer and gives him spiritual life. That is the "new man" we have discussed earlier.

Every human being has a body and a soul. Because of sin, our physical body will die. But that can be fixed. Even though our bodies will lie in a grave for a while, the Father who raised his Son will also raise our body. On judgment day he will rejoin it with our soul, which does not die. With reunited body and soul, believers will then live eternally with God in heaven.

<u>Things to remember:</u>

42. The God of the Bible is a _____ God.
    This means there are _____ persons in
    _____ God.

43. The Holy Spirit _____ in believers and gives them a "new man."

44. On judgment day God will _____ those who have died.

45. Believers will _____ forever with God in heaven.

(Check your answers on page 90.)

After judgment day believers will live with God in heaven. But that is in the future. Until that time we have an obligation to fulfill during our earthly life.

(Read Romans 8:12,13)

[12] Brothers and sisters, we have a duty. Our duty is not to live under the control of our sinful nature. [13] If you live under the control of your sinful nature, you will die. But by the power of the Holy Spirit you can put to death the sins your body commits. Then you will live.

Throughout their life believers always have a sinful nature, the old Adam. This sinful nature wants to lead us into sin. With the Holy Spirit living in us we can and we must resist the sinful desires that still come to us every day. We dare not let them control our life. That leads to death. Evil desires will not be in control if the Holy Spirit guides us.

How does the Holy Spirit guide us? He does so through his Word, the Bible. In fact, he is doing that right now as you read Paul's inspired letter to the Romans. It tells you that Christ has done everything needed for our salvation. He has given us his righteousness as a free gift to be accepted by faith. Out of appreciation for all he has done for us, we will now want to avoid sinning. We will do what pleases God.

(Read Romans 8:14-17)

[14] Those who are led by the Spirit of God are children of God. [15] You didn't receive a spirit that makes you a slave to fear once again. Instead you received the Holy Spirit, who makes you God's child. By the Spirit's power we call God "Abba." Abba means Father. [16] The Spirit himself joins with our spirits. Together they give witness that we are God's children.

[17] As his children, we will receive all that he has for us. We will share what Christ receives. But we must share in his sufferings if we want to share in his glory.

Children in a loving family want to please their parents. The same is true in our spiritual family. Believers are children of their heavenly Father. Paul says, "Those who are led by the Spirit of God are children of God." With the Holy Spirit living in us, we need not be afraid of our heavenly Father. We can affectionately call him "Abba." We can confidently go to him with requests for help and guidance.

But there is another great benefit we have as God's children. We are heirs of our heavenly Father. We will inherit everything that Christ has. Think about it: Jesus is the <u>Son</u> of God. We are <u>children</u> of God. That makes Jesus our brother. We will share in everything that Christ receives. But we need to know that along with all the good things Christ shares with us, we also share in his suffering.

<u>Things to remember:</u>

46. We have a duty to fight against _____.
47. The _____ _____ who lives in us helps us in our fight against sin.
48. Believers are children of _____.
49. Children of God are _____ of Christ.
50. As brothers of Christ we will _____ everything Christ receives.

(Check your answers on page 90.)

Future Glory after Present Suffering

(Read Romans 8:18-22)

[18] What we are suffering now is nothing compared with the glory that will be shown in us.
[19] Everything God created looks forward to the time when his children will appear in their full and final glory. [20] The created world was bound to fail. But that was not the result of its own choice. It was planned that way by the One who made it. God planned [21] to set the created world free. He didn't want it to rot away completely. Instead, he wanted it to have the same glorious freedom that his children have.
[22] We know that all that God created has been groaning. It is in pain as if it were giving birth to a child. The created world continues to groan even now.

As children of God we are brothers of Christ and heirs together with him. We will share in everything he receives. Along with many pleasant things that includes also some suffering. But we are not alone in suffering.

Paul tells us that the natural world around us is also suffering. When Adam and Eve fell into sin, they spoiled the perfect world God created. Nature now feels the effects of man's sin. It longs to get rid of the burden sin causes. Paul writes, "Everything God created looks forward to the time when his children will appear in their full and final glory."

God's children will receive their "full and final glory" on judgment day. Then their bodies and souls will be reunited and they will live forever in heaven. That day will also be a blessing for nature, which is currently groaning in pain. The author doesn't give us any details, but he says God has a plan for removing nature's suffering.

But the main emphasis here is not on nature. This is a section of comfort for suffering Christians.

Things to remember:

51. The sin of humans causes nature to

_____.

52. Nature's suffering will end on _____

_____.

(Check your answers on page 90.)

(Read Romans 8:22b-23)

The created world continues to groan even now. [23] And that's not all. We have the Holy Spirit as the promise of future blessing. But we also groan inside ourselves as we look forward to the time when God will adopt us as full members of his family. Then he will give us everything he has for us. He will raise our bodies and give glory to them.

Nature groans under the burden of people's sin. But nature is not alone. People cause themselves and others lots of trouble and hardship. People also groan in pain. These hardships cause believers to look forward to the time when God will set everything right.

But how do we know that such improvement will happen. First of all, we have such assurance because the Holy Spirit lives in us. Paul says, "We have the Holy Spirit as the promise of future blessing." Sinful people cannot work faith in their heart. That is the work of the Holy Spirit. Because we have faith we know that the Holy Spirit has worked in our hearts. He now lives in us and will bring us future blessings.

A second assurance is God's promise. Jesus told his twelve disciples, "There are many rooms in my Father's house… I am going there to prepare a place for you. If I go and do that, I will come back. And will take you to be with me. Then you will also be with me where I am" (John 14:2-4). Such a promise allows Paul to say that as full members of God's family "he [God] will give us everything he has for us. He will raise our bodies and give glory to them."

Remember that as children of God we are God's heirs.

We will share in everything God has to give. Here two very great blessings are mentioned. God will give us new life by raising us from our graves. That new life in heaven will be lived in a body that has been gloriously changed. What a glorified body will be like we cannot know until we experience it on the Last Day.

Things to remember:

53. Like nature, people also look forward to being freed from _____.

54. This freeing from suffering will take place on

_____ _____.

55. One assurance that believers will be freed from suffering on judgment day is the presence of the

_____ _____ living in them.

56. A second assurance is the _____ Jesus made to prepare a place for us.

57. One blessing of judgment day is that people will _____ from their graves.

58. Another blessing is that believers will rise with a _____ body.

(Check your answers on page 90.)

(Read Romans 8:24-27)

[24] That's the hope we had when we were saved. But hope that can be seen is no hope at all. Who hopes for what he already has? [25] We hope for what we don't have yet. So we are patient as we wait for it.
[26] In the same way, the Holy Spirit helps us when we are weak. We don't know what we should pray for. But the Spirit himself prays for us. He prays with groans too deep for words. [27] God, who looks into our hearts, knows the mind of the Spirit. And the Spirit prays for God's people just as God wants him to pray.

The word "hope" always looks to the future. It speaks of things we don't yet have. It can be understood in two ways.

It can mean a wish for something we are not very sure of getting. For example: we are planning a picnic on a cloudy day. We may say, "I hope it won't rain"—but we are not at all sure the weather will stay dry.

There is another kind of hope. It patiently waits for something it does not yet have but is sure to receive. That kind of hope can be placed on anything God promises. Such hope is basically trust. We could also call it confidence. Faith is trust and confidence in God's promises.

Our new man trusts God's promises. Our old Adam tries to make us doubt them. Sometimes we need help. Paul says, "The Holy Spirit helps us when we are weak." Sometimes we do not know how to pray, or even what to pray for. Then the Holy Spirit steps in. He improves our weak prayers and passes them on to the Father. With the Spirit's help, our prayers become perfect prayers, fully acceptable to our heavenly Father.

Things to remember:

59. Faith is _____ and _____ in
    God's _____.
60. When our prayer life is weak, the _____
    _____ helps us. Such prayers are acceptable to
    our _____ _____.

(Check your answers on page 90.)

(Read Romans 8:28-30)

[28] We know that in all things God works for the good of those who love him. He appointed them to be saved in keeping with his purpose.

[29] God planned that those he had chosen would become like his Son. In that way, Christ will be the first and most honored among many brothers.
[30] And those God has planned for, he has also appointed to be saved. Those he has appointed, he has made right with himself. To those he has made right with himself, he has given his glory.

Writing to the Ephesians Paul says, "God chose us to belong to Christ before the world was created. He chose us to be holy and without blame in his eyes" (Ephesians 1:4). Before we were born—even before the world was created—God planned to send his Son to save us sinners. Here in his letter to the Romans, Paul does not describe God's plan. He simply tells us what effect it has on our lives. He says, "We know that in all things God works for the good of those who love him. He appointed them to be saved in keeping with his purpose."

God has a plan for us. Everything is under control. From eternity God planned to send his Son as the world's Savior from sin. Some 2000 years ago he sent Jesus Christ to suffer and die in your place. Now at the present time he is inviting you to believe that truth. In the future he will glorify you in heaven. Such glorious promises lead Paul to ask a series of questions.

Things to remember:

61. From _____ God planned our salvation.
62. At the present time God invites us to _____.
63. In the future God will _____.
(Check your answers at page 90.)

(Read Romans 8:31-34)

[31] What should we say then? Since God is on our side, who can be against us? [32] God did not spare his own Son. He gave him up for us all. Then won't he also freely give us everything else?
[33] Who can bring any charge against God's chosen ones? God makes us right with himself. [34] Who can sentence us to death? Christ Jesus is at the right hand of God and is also praying for us. He died. More than that, he was raised to life.

Question One: "Since God is on our side, who can be against us? *Answer:* NO ONE! Since God has already given us his dearest possession, his own Son, isn't he going to protect us and give us everything we need?

Question Two: Who can bring any charge against God's chosen ones. *Answer:* NO ONE! God is the judge. He has declared us righteous.

Question Three: Who can sentence us to death? *Answer:* NO ONE! Christ died but was raised to life. He now lives with God and serves as our defense attorney.

Something to remember:

64. Since God is for us, _____ _____ can
    successfully be against us.
(Check your answer on page 90.)

(Read Romans 8:35-39)

[35] Who can separate us from Christ's love? Can trouble or hard times or harm or hunger? Can nakedness or danger or war? [36] It is written,
"Because of you, we face death all day long.
We are considered as sheep to be killed." —(*Psalm 44:22*)
[37] No! In all these things we will do even more than win! We owe it all to Christ, who has loved us.
[38] I am absolutely sure that not even death or life can separate us from God's love. Not even angels or demons, the present or the future, or any powers can do that. [39] Not even the highest places or the lowest, or anything else in all creation can do that. Nothing at all can ever separate us from God's love because of what Christ Jesus our Lord has done.

Fourth Question: Who can separate us from Christ's love? To answer that question Paul lists seven bad things (trouble / hard times / harm / hunger / nakedness / danger / war). All of these are serious. They cause major problems. But they can not separate the believer from Christ.

Look at verses 38 and 39. Notice that Paul emphasizes the same point by adding ten (10) more things. None of these can separate the believer from Christ either. Nothing in all creation can do that.

Regarding this great and comforting truth Paul can say, "I am absolutely sure." That is faith speaking. Remember we have said faith is trust and confidence in God's promises. Faith is not a good work that earns us something. It is not the cause of our salvation. Faith merely receives what God has done for us. Paul teaches that truth with his closing statement, "Nothing at all can ever separate us from God's love <u>because of what Christ Jesus our Lord has done</u>." There will always be troubles in our life, but God's love in Christ gives us strength for present problems and makes us confident of future glory.

Things to remember-Answers

1. faith; 2. Christ; 3. dead; 4. new life; 5. for, to; 6. dead; 7. sin, bad things, pleases; 8. law, saved; 9. gift; 10. live a new life; 11. Baptism, Word of God/Bible; 12. master; 13. sin; 14. dying for sin; 15. good, please; 16. living; 17. has died; 18. law; 19. law; 20. died; 21. law; 22. Spirit; 23. God; 24. sin, die; 25. sin, savior; 26. good; 27. sinful; 28. get control; 29. new man; 30. good things; 31. sinful; 32. old Adam; 33. bad things; 34. fight; 35. Christ; 36. keep; 37. law, weak; 38. offering; 39. forgiveness; 40. Spirit; 41. thank; 42. triune, three, one; 43. lives; 44. raise; 45. live; 46. sin; 47. Holy Spirit; 48. God; 49. brothers; 50. share; 51. suffer; 52. judgment day; 53. suffering; 54. judgment day; 55. Holy Spirit; 56. promise; 57. rise; 58. glorified; 59. trust, confidence, promises; 60. Holy Spirit, heavenly Father; 61. eternity; 62. believe; 63. glorify you in heaven; 64. NO ONE.

TEST - Righteous Through Faith:
A Study of the Epistle to the Romans

Section 4
Please review the "Things to remember."

1. Through baptism the Holy Spirit works _____ in the baptized person's heart.
   Baptism joins us with _____.

2. With Christ we died to _____ in our baptism. We will now try to avoid doing _____ _____ and we will try to do what _____ God.

3. The law shows us what _____ expects of people.

4. The law is good because it shows us our _____ and our need for a _____ from sin.

5. Coming to faith gives the believer a _____ _____. This new man wants to do _____ _____.

6. Every believer still has a _____ nature. This sinful nature is often called our _____ _____.

7. Every day the "new man" and the old Adam _____ with each other.

8. God sent his Son to be born as a human so he could be an _____ for sin.

9. Christ's death earned _____ for the sins of the whole world.

10. The God of the Bible is a _____ God. This means there are _____ persons in _____ God.

11. On judgment day God will _____ those who have died. Believers will _____ forever with God in heaven.

12. Faith is _____ and _____ in God's _____.

13. When our prayer life is weak, the _____ _____ helps us. Such prayers are acceptable to our _____ _____.

14. From _____ God planned our salvation.

15. At the present time God invites us to _____

16. In the future God will _____.

17. Since God is for us, _____ _____ can successfully be against us.

(Check your answers on page 192.)

RIGHTEOUS
THROUGH FAITH

SECTION 5:
God's Justice and Mercy in Dealing with Jews and Gentiles

Romans 9:1 – 11:36

Righteous Through Faith:
A Study of the Epistle to the Romans

SECTION FIVE:
God's Justice and Mercy in Dealing with Jews and Gentiles

God's Justice and Mercy in Dealing with Jews and Gentiles (9:1–11:36)

Paul was an orthodox Jewish rabbi until Jesus met him on the road to Damascus and called him to be a Christian missionary. It could look like Paul had turned against his fellow Jews. Paul strongly denies this. He very much wants his fellow Jews to receive salvation through faith in Christ. He would even be willing to give up his own salvation if that would help them.

(Read Romans 9:1-3)

[1] I speak the truth in Christ. I am not lying. My mind tells me that what I say is true. It is guided by the Holy Spirit. [2] My heart is full of sorrow. My sadness never ends. [3] I am so concerned about my people, who are members of my own race. I am ready to be cursed, if that would help them. I am even willing to be separated from Christ.

Paul notes that over the centuries God gave his chosen people, the Jews, many advantages. These include: adoption as God's children; special covenants, the law given through Moses, the temple and its worship. But the biggest gift was the promise that the Savior of the world would be born of them

(Read Romans 9:4,5)

[4] They are the people of Israel. They have been adopted as God's children. God's glory belongs to them. So do the covenants. They received the law. They were taught to worship in the temple. They were given the promises.

94

Moses raises a bronze snake as a picture of Christ.

[5] The founders of our nation belong to them. Christ comes from their family line. He is God over all. May he always be praised! Amen.

At the time of Paul's writing to the Romans most of the Jews (also called "Israel") were rejecting his Christian message. Paul stresses that this is not God's fault. God's Word has not failed. His promises are still good. The fault lies with Israel's unbelief. They do not look in faith to the promised Savior. That leads Paul to say, "Not everyone in the family line of Israel really belongs to Israel." In other words, not everyone descended from Abraham is by that physical connection a child of God.

Abraham and his servant girl Hagar had a son Ishmael, but he was not the son God had promised. God's promise rested on a son to be born of Abraham and his wife Sarah. That son was Isaac. Both Ishmael and Isaac were sons of Abraham, but God chose Isaac to be the fulfillment of promise.

(Read Romans 9:6-9)

[6] Their condition does not mean that God's word has failed. Not everyone in the family line of Israel really belongs to Israel. [7] Not everyone in Abraham's family line is really his child. Not at all! Scripture says, "Your family line will continue through Isaac."—(*Genesis 21:12*)
[8] In other words, God's children are not just Abraham's natural children. Instead, they are the children God promised to him. They are the ones considered to be Abraham's children. [9] God promised, "I will return at the appointed time. Sarah will have a son."—(*Genesis 18:10,14*)

Throughout this letter Paul stresses that salvation is by grace. "Grace" means it is a gift given by God's free choice. There is no human merit involved. It is not because a person has done something good to earn God's favor. He illustrates this truth with an incident in the life of Isaac and his wife Rebekah.

A servant brings Rebekah to Isaac.

This pious couple was expecting twins. Before they were born, God informed the mother, "The older son will serve the younger." That was an unusual arrangement. By Jewish custom, the first-born usually had some advantages. In this particular case it involved carrying on the line of the Savior previously promised to Abraham and Isaac. Here God chose to have that special privilege given to the younger twin Jacob rather than his older brother Esau. The decision rested purely on God's choice, not human actions.

Paul uses this as support for his statement, "So it doesn't depend on what we want or do. It depends on God's mercy."

(Read Romans 9:11-16)

[10] And that's not all. Rebekah's children had the same father. He was our father Isaac.

[11] Here is what happened. Rebekah's twins had not even been born. They hadn't done anything good or bad yet. So they show that God's purpose is based firmly on his free choice. [12] It was not because of anything they did but because of God's choice. So Rebekah was told, "The older son will serve the younger one."—(*Genesis 25:23*) [13] It is written, "I chose Jacob instead of Esau."—(*Malachi 1:2,3*)

[14] What should we say then? Is God unfair? Not at all! [15] He said to Moses,

"I will have mercy on whom I have mercy.
I will show love to those I love."—(*Exodus 33:19*)

[16] So it doesn't depend on what we want or do. It depends on God's mercy.

God has the right to show mercy where he wants. He also has the right to take away his mercy. People's life on earth is often called their "time of grace." If unbelievers insist on disobeying God and doubting his promises, God does not forcibly stop them. But he may end their time of grace by withdrawing his mercy from them. That is what happened to the Egyptian ruler Pharaoh.

When God sent Moses to ask Pharaoh to release the Jewish nation from slavery in Egypt, Pharaoh repeatedly hardened his heart and refused. When Pharaoh insisted on opposing God, then God eventually hardened his heart. God showed his power and holiness by ending Pharaoh's time of grace.

A holy God has the right both to show mercy to penitent sinners and to show his power by withdrawing his mercy from stubborn unbelievers.

(Read Romans 9:17,18)

[17] In Scripture, God says to Pharaoh, "I had a special reason for making you king. I decided to use you to show my power. I wanted my name to become known everywhere on earth."—(*Exodus 9:16*) [18] So God does what he wants to do. He shows mercy to one person and makes another stubborn.

Here Paul expects an objection. Someone is going to say, "If it is all God's doing, what difference does it make what we do?" Paul gives two answers. The short answer is, "Don't talk back to God!"

The fuller answer is: The situation is parallel to the relationship between a potter and the clay he works with. The clay does not tell the potter what kind of vessel it wants to be. And on a spiritual level, creatures do not control the Creator.

Paul now follows with two questions of his own. In verse 22 he asks, "Is God doing something wrong if, after putting up with evil people, he chooses to show his anger against them?" The answer, of course is, "There is nothing wrong with that."

In verse 23 he asks a parallel question. "Is God doing something wrong if he chooses to show mercy to people he has prepared to receive his glory?" The answer again is, "There is nothing wrong with that."

(Read Romans 9:19-23)

[19] One of you will say to me, "Then why does God still blame us? Who can oppose what he wants to do?" [20] But you are a mere man. So who are you to talk back to God? Scripture says, "Can what is made say to the one who made it, 'Why did you make me like this?' "—(*Isaiah 29:16; 45:9*) [21] Isn't the potter free to make different kinds of pots out of the same lump of clay? Some are for special purposes. Others are for ordinary use. [22] What if God chose to show his great anger? What if he chose to make his power known? That is why he put up with people he was angry with. They had been made to be destroyed. [23] What if he did that to show the riches of his glory to others? Those are the people he shows his mercy to. He had prepared them to receive his glory.

Paul has established that God may show mercy to whomever he pleases. Then Paul announces to his readers, "We are those people to whom God has shown mercy. He chose us. And we are not all Jews. Many of us are Gentiles."

Having Gentiles in the church should not be a great surprise. Through the prophet Hosea God prophesied that long ago. The Gentiles, who formerly were not God's chosen people, are now objects of his mercy in the New Testament church.

On the other hand, the chosen nation of the Old Testament, the Jewish people, have mostly rejected God's mercy. They are missing out on God's salvation. This too is exactly what the prophet Isaiah foretold many years before. He said, "The number of people from Israel may be like the sand of the sea. But only a few of them will be saved."

(Read Romans 9:24-29)

[24] We are those people. He has chosen us. We do not come only from the Jewish race. Many of us are not Jews. [25] God says in Hosea,

"I will call those who are not my people 'my people.'

I will call the one who is not my loved one 'my loved one.' "—(*Hosea 2:23*) [26] He also says,

"Once it was said to them,

'You are not my people.'
In that very place they will be called 'children of the living God.' " —
(*Hosea 1:10*)
[27] Isaiah cries out concerning Israel. He says,
"The number of people from Israel may be like the sand by the sea.
But only a few of them will be saved.
[28] The Lord will carry out his sentence.
He will be quick to carry it out on earth, once and for all." —(*Isaiah 10:22,23*)
[29] Earlier Isaiah had said,
"The Lord who rules over all
left us children and grandchildren.
If he hadn't, we would have become like Sodom.
We would have been like Gomorrah." —(*Isaiah 1:9*)

What caused this great change? While the Gentiles were lost in sin and doomed to death, God came to them in his mercy. They weren't looking for salvation, but God brought them his message of free forgiveness and life in Christ. The Gentiles believed that message. By faith they accepted it and became children of God and heirs of eternal life.

On the other hand, very many of the Jews were actively looking for a way to be saved. They were looking for a law that could make them right with God. But they didn't find it. Why not? Because they did not look for righteousness by faith. They tried to get it by working for it. Preferring their own righteousness over that earned for them by Christ, they rejected God's mercy. They stumbled over Christ like a rock in their path.

(Read Romans 9:30-33)

[30] What should we say then? Those who aren't Jews did not look for a way to be right with God. But they found it by having faith. [31] Israel did look for a law that could make them right with God. But they didn't find it.
[32] Why not? Because they didn't look for it by faith. They tried to get it by working for it. They tripped over the stone that causes people to trip

The wise men worship Jesus.

and fall. [33] It is written,

"Look! In Zion I am laying a stone that causes people to trip.
It is a rock that makes them fall.
The one who trusts in him will never be put to shame."—(*Isaiah 8:14; 28:16*)

Things to remember:

1. Paul is a Jew who is very concerned about his fellow-Jews who do not _____.
2. God can show _____ to whomever he wants.
3. In Old Testament times God showed his mercy in a special way to _____ by choosing them as his _____ _____.
4. In New Testament times God is showing his mercy in a special way to _____.
5. Gentiles become children of God by _____.
6. God's promises to the Jewish nation are still good. But many Jews are missing out on salvation because they want to _____ it by their own _____ rather than accept it as a _____ from God.

(Check your answers on page 119.)

Romans 10

Chapter ten begins much like chapter nine did. In the opening verses the apostle expresses his deep sorrow that so many of his Jewish countrymen are missing out on salvation. These Jews are earnest people who want to serve God, but they are going about it the wrong way. They are trying to get right with God by keeping the law. They want to earn salvation by doing what God expects.

And it's true, Moses does say, "The one who does those things will live by them." The problem is that people are born sinful. They cannot keep the law perfectly, as a holy God rightly demands. They earn God's anger rather than his approval by their imperfect keeping of the law.

God's law has to be kept, but thankfully there is another way that can be done. That way is to have someone else keep the law in the sinner's place. And that is exactly what Christ did. He fulfilled the law for us. By accepting his righteousness through faith we now look perfectly righteous to our holy God. We look as though we had kept the law.

(Read Romans 10:1-4)

[1] Brothers and sisters, with all my heart I long for the people of Israel to be saved. I pray to God for them. [2] I can give witness about them that they really want to serve God. But how they are trying to do it is not based on what they know.

[3] They didn't know how God makes people right with himself. They tried to get right with God in their own way. They didn't do it in God's way.

[4] Christ has completed the law. So now everyone who believes can be right with God.

God's law tells us what he wants us to do. Children of God want to do what pleases their heavenly Father. But as Paul points out, the way to do what God requires must begin by having faith in him.

Having faith does not require some kind of hard work on our part. It does not require us to get Christ down from heaven. We do not have to raise him from the grave. It is much easier than that. Faith comes by hearing and accepting God's Word.

That Word is readily available. Paul quotes from the Old Testament book of Deuteronomy when he says "The word is near you. It's in your mouth and in your heart." Then he adds, "That means the word we are preaching."

Still today you are reading what Paul in this letter "preached" to the Romans. Still today the Holy Spirit invites you to put your faith in that saving message.

(Read Romans 10:5-8)

5 Moses explained how the law could help a person do what God requires. He said, "The one who does those things will live by them."—(*Leviticus 18:5*)

6 But the way to do what God requires must begin by having faith in him. Scripture says, "Do not say in your heart, 'Who will go up into heaven?'"—(*Deuteronomy 30:12*) That means to go up into heaven and bring Christ down. 7 "And do not say, 'Who will go down into the grave?'"—(*Deuteronomy 30:13*) That means to bring Christ up from the dead. 8 But what does it say? "The word is near you. It's in your mouth and in your heart."—(*Deuteronomy 30:14*) That means the word we are preaching. You must put your faith in it.

The Holy Spirit works though the Word. God's Word (the Bible) has the power to bring about a change in a person. It affects two things: a person's heart and his mouth. Paul says, "With your heart you believe." That is the big change. God's Word makes a person a believer. It leads him to believe God's promises. It convinces him to trust in Christ's righteousness and not in his own.

We cannot look into someone's heart and see faith, but faith shows itself in a different way. Paul says, "With your mouth you say that Jesus is Lord." When a believer's heart trusts in Christ, then his mouth can say, "Jesus is my Lord." Calling Jesus "Lord" is saying, "I trust him for my salvation."

Note again, faith is not a work. It is not something a believer does. It is trust and confidence in God's mercy. Faith merely accepts what God gives as a free gift.

(Read Romans 10:9-11)

9 Say with your mouth, "Jesus is Lord." Believe in your heart that God raised him from the dead. Then you will be saved. 10 With your heart you believe and are made right with God. With your mouth you say that Jesus is Lord. And so you are saved. 11 Scripture says, "The one who trusts in him will never be put to shame."—(*Isaiah 28:16*)

There is only one plan of salvation. That is by faith in Christ Jesus. For that reason Paul can say it makes no difference whether a person is a Jew or a Gentile. The same plan of salvation works for everyone because the Lord richly blesses everyone who calls on him.

"Calling on the Lord" is an important term. It is another way of saying: With his mouth a believer expresses the faith he has in his heart.

What makes such calling on the Lord possible? Paul lists the steps involved. Before a person can call on the Lord, he must have heard God's Word. To hear God's Word, someone had to "preach" it to him. Before going out to preach the Word, the preacher had to be sent. God does the sending.

Paul is talking about the important service messengers of the gospel do when they share God's Word with us. We should honor and respect teachers, preachers and chaplains who bring God's Word to us. Then we will agree with the prophet Isaiah who wrote; "How beautiful are the feet of those who bring good news!"

(Read Romans 10:12-15)

[12] There is no difference between those who are Jews and those who are not. The same Lord is Lord of all. He richly blesses everyone who calls on him. [13] Scripture says, "Everyone who calls on the name of the Lord will be saved."—(*Joel 2:32*)

[14] How can they call on him unless they believe in him? How can they believe in him unless they hear about him? How can they hear about him unless someone preaches to them? [15] And how can anyone preach without being sent? It is written, "How beautiful are the feet of those who bring good news!"—(*Isaiah 52:7*)

Throughout the Old Testament God sent prophets (preachers) to his chosen people Israel. Repeatedly he invited them to trust in the promised Savior who would be born of their nation.

Paul and Barnabas preach God's Word.

Israel heard the message, but they did not believe it. When most of the Jewish nation rejected Christ as their Savior, God in his mercy took the message of salvation to the Gentiles. Paul was sent by God as a missionary to the Gentiles. Many Gentiles accepted his message. The New Testament Christian church became largely a Gentile church.

But God did not forget Israel. Moses tells us of God's plan. God says, "I will use people who are not a nation to make you jealous." The "people who are not a nation" are the Gentiles. God poured out all the blessings of salvation on them. God's intent was that when the Jewish nation saw all these blessings going to the Gentiles, the Jewish people would become envious. Hopefully out of "jealousy" they would join in with the Gentiles to also share in the salvation earned by Christ.

Did the plan work? It did with the Gentiles. Isaiah quotes God as saying, "I was found by those who were not trying to find me. I made myself known to those who were not asking for me."

The plan was less successful with the Jewish nation. Of them God has to say, "All day long I have held out my hands. I have held them out to a stubborn people who do not obey me."

(Read Romans 10:16-21)

[16] But not all the people of Israel accepted the good news. Isaiah says, "Lord, who has believed our message?"—(*Isaiah 53:1*) [17] So faith comes from hearing the message. And the message that is heard is the word of Christ.
[18] But I ask, "Didn't the people of Israel hear?" Of course they did. It is written,
"Their voice has gone out into the whole earth.
Their words have gone out from one end of the world to the other."
—(*Psalm 19:4*)
[19] Again I ask, "Didn't Israel understand?" First, Moses says,
"I will use people who are not a nation to make you jealous.

I will use a nation that has no understanding to make you angry."—(*Deuteronomy 32:21*)

[20] Then Isaiah boldly speaks about what God says. God said,

"I was found by those who were not trying to find me.

I made myself known to those who were not asking for me."—(*Isaiah 65:1*) [21] But Isaiah also speaks about what God says concerning Israel. God said,

"All day long I have held out my hands.

I have held them out to a stubborn people who do not obey me."—(*Isaiah 65:2*)

Things to remember:

7. There is only _____ plan of salvation.
8. This plan of salvation works for both _____ and _____.
9. To come to faith a person must hear _____ _____.
10. _____ sends out preachers of his word.
11. In New Testament times God gave his blessings to the _____ in order to make the _____ jealous. God hoped that Jews also would accept his salvation.
12. Many of the _____ accepted Christ as their Savior. Only a few _____ accepted Christ.

(Check your answers on page 119.)

Romans 11

Paul has repeatedly expressed his sorrow over the fact that in general the Jewish nation has rejected Jesus Christ as their Savior. They are not on the way to heaven. In his sorrow he wonders why that has happened. He asks, "Did God turn his back on his people?" Paul answers his own question by saying "Not at all." He gives two reasons for that negative answer.

First of all, Paul offers himself as exhibit A. He is a Jew. If God were no longer saving Jews, then Paul could not be saved. But God not only chose him for salvation, he even appointed him as an apostle, trusting him to preach the gospel. Clearly God still accepts Jews.

Paul gives a second reason for saying God has not abandoned the Jewish nation. There are more believers in Israel than one can see. The situation is similar to what happened in the prophet Elijah's day. Because he could not see faith in people's heart, Elijah thought there were no believers left in Israel. God had to tell him "I have kept 7,000 people for myself."

Since faith in the heart is invisible, Paul can say in regard to the Jews of his own time, "Some are also faithful today. They have been chosen by God's grace."

(Read Romans 11:1-6)

[1] So here is what I ask. Did God turn his back on his people? Not at all! I myself belong to Israel. I am one of Abraham's children. I am from the tribe of Benjamin. [2] God didn't turn his back on his people. After all, he chose them.

Don't you know what Scripture says about Elijah? He complained to God about Israel. [3] He said, "Lord, they have killed your prophets. They have torn down your altars. I'm the only one left. And they are trying to kill me."—(*1 Kings 19:10,14*)

[4] How did God answer him? God said, "I have kept 7,000 people for myself. They have not bowed down to Baal."—(*1 Kings 19:18*)

[5] Some are also faithful today. They have been chosen by God's grace. [6] And if they are chosen by grace, it is no longer a matter of working for it. If it were, grace wouldn't be grace anymore.

Paul draws the conclusion that among the Jewish people there are still some believers, even though their faith is invisible. He can be sure of it because they have been chosen by God's grace. But such a statement can easily raise the logical question: If God has chosen some to be saved, what about the others? Are there some poor souls who never had a chance? We need to be careful how we answer that question. Even Paul's statement in verse 7 here needs to be read carefully.

Paul addresses the matter of God's choice with the question, "What should we say then?" He provides the answer, "Israel did not receive what they wanted so badly. But those who were chosen did. God made the rest of them stubborn."

Scripture clearly says that God wants all people to be saved. Jesus is rightly called the Lamb of God who takes away the sin of the world. Go back to chapter 10 verse 21 in this letter to the Romans. There we heard God saying, "All day long I have held out my hands. I have held them out to a stubborn people who do not obey me." Clearly God is inviting Israel to be saved. God is not rejecting Israel. They are rejecting him.

Paul has previously referred to Pharaoh, king of Egypt at Moses' time. When he refused to let God's people go and repeatedly hardened his heart, it eventually came to the time when God hardened Pharaoh's heart.

Likewise, when Israel refused to believe God's gracious promises and rejected his invitation, it eventually came to the time when they no longer could believe. That is the sad state Paul describes by quoting Old Testament passages that speak of God withdrawing his grace from stubborn unbelievers. Scripture uses pictures like minds darkened so they cannot understand spiritual truths, eyes that cannot see and ears that cannot hear.

God is a loving and merciful God, but he is also just and holy. He graciously forgives repentant sinners. He severely punishes stubborn and unbelieving sinners who reject his grace.

(Read Romans 11:7-10)

---

[7] What should we say then? Israel did not receive what they wanted so badly. But those who were chosen did. God made the rest of them stubborn.

[8] It is written,
"God made it hard for them to understand.
   He gave them eyes that could not see.
   He gave them ears that could not hear.
And they are still like that today."—(*Deuteronomy 29:4; Isaiah 29:10*)
[9] David says,
"Let their feast be a trap and a snare.
   Let it make Israel trip and fall. Let Israel get what's coming to them.
[10] Let their eyes grow dark so they can't see.
   Let their backs be bent forever."—(*Psalm 69:22,23*)

The Old Testament passages just quoted paint a bleak picture for Israel. Their minds do not understand spiritual things. Their eyes do not see; their ears do not hear. Is there any hope for Israel? Paul says, Yes there is! In fact, he sees a very positive outcome from the current situation.

When Israel rejected God's message of salvation by faith in Christ, God took it away from them and gave it to the Gentiles. Paul says in verses 11 and 12, "Because Israel sinned, those who aren't Jews can be saved…. Israel's sin brought riches to the world. Their loss brought riches to the non-Jews."

Paul is an apostle bringing "riches" to "non-Jews" (Gentiles). He works very hard at converting as many Gentiles as possible. This may have the effect of making the Jews jealous of their Gentile neighbors who are now getting all the "riches" that God gives to believers in Christ. Paul tells his Gentile readers, "I hope somehow to stir up my own people to want what you have. Perhaps I can save some of them."

Paul is genuinely concerned about his Jewish countrymen. He sincerely hopes that this attempt to draw Jews into the Christian church will work. But he does not expect it to win over all of them. His hope is that perhaps he can save some of them.

(Read Romans 11:11-15)

[11] Again, here is what I ask. They didn't trip and fall once and for all time, did they? Not at all! Because Israel sinned, those who aren't Jews can be saved. That will make Israel jealous of them. [12] Israel's sin brought riches to the world. Their loss brought riches to the non-Jews. What greater riches will come when all Israel turns to God!
[13] I am talking to you who are not Jews. I am the apostle to the non-Jews. So I think the work I do for God and others is very important.
[14] I hope somehow to stir up my own people to want what you have. Perhaps I can save some of them. [15] When they were not accepted, it became possible for the whole world to be brought back to God. So what will happen when they are accepted? It will be like life from the dead.

Because Israel in general refused to accept the Christian message, God took it from them and gave it to the Gentiles. Many of them came to faith. Being the majority in the Christian church, Gentiles could very easily become proud. They could think they were now God's chosen people and Israel was excluded.

The Romans who received Paul's letter were a mixed group. Most of them were Gentiles, but there were also some Jews among them. In this section of his letter Paul is speaking directly to his Gentile readers. Recall that three verses previous (v. 13) Paul stated, "I am talking to you who are not Jews."

Because the Gentiles have received the gospel while Israel has largely lost it does not give Gentiles any reason to boast or become proud. Paul illustrates the situation by taking an example from the olive orchard.

In an orchard branches from fruit trees can be "grafted" (joined) onto healthy rootstock. Paul compares Gentiles to "wild" olive branches. Israel is like a cultivated or "tame" olive tree. God's taking Gentiles into his New Testament church is like grafting "wild" branches into the good rootstock consisting of the Old Testament promise he originally gave to Israel.

Paul warns his Gentile readers, "You have no reason to become proud. The branches do not support the root. The root gives life to the branches." For the same thought, remember Jesus telling the Samaritan woman at Jacob's well, "Salvation is from the Jews" (John 4:22).

(Read Romans 11:16-18)

[16] The first handful of dough that is offered is holy. This makes all of the dough holy.

If the root is holy, so are the branches.

[17] Some of the natural branches have been broken off. You are a wild olive branch. But you have been joined to the tree with the other branches. Now you enjoy the life-giving sap of the olive tree root. [18] So don't think you are better than the other branches. Remember, you don't give life to the root. The root gives life to you.

Here the author of the letter expects an objection from a Gentile reader, "You will say, 'Some branches were broken off so that I could be joined to the tree.'" Paul agrees with that statement, but he uses it to repeat an important truth: God's choosing the Gentiles is not because of any merit in them. It is purely by God's grace. It is a free gift accepted through faith.

But there is a second lesson to learn from all this. Israel's loss because of their unbelief is a stern reminder how serious God is about people accepting salvation on his terms. God offers salvation through faith in Christ. Rejecting that Savior results in severe punishment for the unbeliever.

There is a useful reminder here also for us. Think about how kind God is to believers. Think about how firm he is in dealing with unbelievers.

(Read Romans 11:19-22)

[19] You will say, "Some branches were broken off so that I could be joined to the tree." [20] That's true. But they were broken off because they didn't

believe. You stand only because you do believe. So don't be proud. Be afraid. [21] God didn't spare the natural branches. He won't spare you either. [22] Think about how kind God is! Also think about how firm he is! He was hard on those who stopped following him. But he is kind to you. So you must continue to live in his kindness. If you don't, you also will be cut off.

God is a stern judge of unbelievers who choose to reject Christ. But that does not mean God wants them to be lost. If they come to faith, they can again be "grafted" into God's "tree." In fact, humanly speaking it should be easier to graft in Jews than Gentiles.

Paul explains: The usual procedure in grafting is to graft in good "tame" branches. But see what God has done here. He has taken "wild" branches (Gentiles) and brought them into his Church. If God can work with normally unproductive "wild" branches, he can certainly join the "natural" branches (Jews) back in also.

(Read Romans 11:23,24)

[23] If the people of Israel do not continue in their unbelief, they will again be joined to the tree. God is able to join them to the tree again.
[24] After all, weren't you [Gentiles] cut from a wild olive tree? Weren't you joined to an olive tree that was taken care of? And wasn't that the opposite of how things should be done? How much more easily will the natural branches [Jews] be joined to their own olive tree!

In this next section Paul tells his Gentile readers that he is sharing a "mystery" with them. This is to keep them from becoming proud.

When Paul uses the term "mystery" he does not mean something that is mysterious or strange. Rather, it is a truth that needs to be explained so that it will be understood correctly. There is a situation that Paul wants his Gentile readers to be perfectly clear on. Even though "part of Israel has refused to obey God," God has not given up on Israel.

Some of them will be saved. Gentiles are not the only objects of God's grace.

Paul has been very plain in describing the problem of Israel's unbelief. For example, in chapter 9, verse 27 he quoted the prophet Isaiah saying, "The number of people from Israel may be like the sand by the sea, but only a few of them will be saved." Earlier in that same chapter (verse 6) he stated, "Not everyone in the family line of Israel really belongs to Israel." Just because someone is an Israelite, a physical descendant of Abraham, does not mean he is a spiritual Israelite, a child of God on the way to heaven.

Not all physical Israelites are spiritual Israel, but those Israelites who are spiritual Israel will certainly be saved. That allows Paul to say here in verse 26, "And so all [spiritual] Israel will be saved."

(Read Romans 11:25-27)

[25] Brothers and sisters, here is a mystery I want you to understand. It will keep you from being proud. Part of Israel has refused to obey God. That will continue until the full number of non-Jews has entered God's kingdom. [26] And so all [spiritual] Israel will be saved. It is written,

"The One who saves will come from Mount Zion.

He will remove sin from Jacob.

[27] Here is my covenant with them.

I will take away their sins."—(*Isaiah 59:20,21; 27:9; Jeremiah 31:33,34*)

Now Paul speaks more directly about the mystery he mentioned previously. Keep in mind that in biblical language a "mystery" is something that has to be explained for people to see and understand. The remarkable thing Paul here explains to his readers is how God has used two bad things to work together so as to bring great blessings for both parties.

In Old Testament times the Israelites were God's chosen people. God gave them special blessings and promises, including the promise of a Savior. But when that Savior was born, they rejected him and his saving message. So God took the message away from them. This was a terrible loss for Israel!

The Gentiles were not the chosen people of the Old Testament. They were wicked people. They lived in all kinds of sins, including idolatry and sexual immorality. Their life was a mess! But when God took the gospel message away from the Jews, he had it preached to the Gentiles. They believed the message. Their lives were totally changed by coming to faith and learning about forgiveness of sins in Christ. Now they could look forward to eternal life with God in heaven. Israel's loss was a huge "win" for the Gentiles.

But God did not intend for that win to stay only with the Gentiles. When Gentiles became the majority in the Christian church, the Jewish nation saw all the blessings that the Gentiles were enjoying. Out of "jealousy" some were moved to want to share in these blessings too. For Jews to share in the gospel blessings was still possible, because God does not go back on his promises. In this way many Jews eventually accepted God's promises and shared in God's gift of salvation.

The "mystery" Paul explains is how a gracious God could take two bad situations and turn both of them into positive gains.

Paul sums this up in two verses of his letter. To the Gentiles he says, "At one time you did not obey God. But now you have received mercy because Israel did not obey." Of the Jews he says, "In the same way, Israel has not been obeying God. But now they receive mercy because of God's mercy to you."

(Read Romans 11:28-32)

28 As far as the good news is concerned, the people of Israel are enemies. That is for your good. But as far as God's choice is concerned, the people

of Israel are loved. That is because of God's promises to the founders of our nation. [29] God does not take back his gifts. He does not change his mind about those he has chosen.

[30] At one time you did not obey God. But now you have received mercy because Israel did not obey. [31] In the same way, Israel has not been obeying God. But now they receive mercy because of God's mercy to you. [32] God has found everyone guilty of not obeying him. So now he can have mercy on everyone.

How God could take two bad situations and turn both of them into "wins" is something no human being could ever have planned or carried out. That could come only from a gracious and merciful God. In wonder and amazement Paul bursts into a four-verse song of praise.

(Read Romans 11:33-36)

[33] How very rich are God's wisdom and knowledge!
  How he judges is more than we can understand!
  The way he deals with people is more than we can know!
[34] "Who can ever know what is in the Lord's mind?
  Or who can ever give him advice?"—(*Isaiah 40:13*)
[35] "Has anyone ever given anything to God,
  so that God has to pay him back?"—(*Job 41:11*)
[36] All things come from him.
  All things are directed by him.
  All things are for his good.
  May God be given the glory forever! Amen.

Things to remember:

13. Paul's letter to the Romans is written to a mixed audience of Jews and Gentiles. In chapter 11 he is speaking directly to _____.

14. In this chapter Paul compares God's Church to an olive tree. The trunk and root of the tree are a picture of the

_____ _____.

15. The_____ are pictured as wild olive branches joined (grafted) into the tree.

16. If God can join wild branches (_____) into the tree (Church), then he can also bring the natural branches (_____) back in.

17. In biblical language a "mystery" is something that has to be explained to people. The mystery Paul explains in chapter 11 is how God has shown _____ to both _____ and _____.

18. When Israel rejected God's message of a Savior, God sent it to the _____.

19. When the Jews saw God's blessings going to the Gentiles, they became _____ and wanted to _____.

(Check your answers on page 119.)

Things to remember-Answers

1. believe in Christ; 2. mercy; 3. Jews, special people; 4. Gentiles; 5. faith;
6. earn, works, gift; 7. one; 8. Jews, Gentiles; 9. God's Word; 10; God;
11. Gentiles, Jews; 12. Gentiles, Jews; 13. Gentiles; 14. Jewish nation;
15. Gentiles; 16. Gentiles, Jews; 17. mercy, Jews, Gentiles; 18.Gentiles;
19. jealous, share in God's blessings.

**TEST - Righteous Through Faith:
A Study of the Epistle to the Romans**

Section 5

Please review the "Things to remember."

1. Paul is a Jew who is very concerned about his fellow-Jews who do not _____.

2. In Old Testament times God showed his mercy in a special way to _____ by choosing them as his _____ _____.

3. In New Testament times God is showing his mercy in a special way to _____.

4. God's promises to the Jewish nation are still good. But many Jews are missing out on salvation because they want to _____ it by their own _____ rather than accept it as a _____ from God.

5. In New Testament times God gave his blessings to the _____ in order to make the _____ jealous. God hoped that Jews also would accept his salvation.

6. In chapter 11 Paul compares God's Church to an olive tree. The trunk and root of the tree are a picture of the _____ _____.

7. The _____ are pictured as wild olive branches joined (grafted) into the tree.

8. In biblical language a "mystery" is something that has to be explained to people. The mystery Paul explains in chapter 11 is how God has shown _____ to both _____ and _____.

(Check your answers on page 192.)

RIGHTEOUS
THROUGH FAITH

Righteous Through Faith:
A Study of the Epistle to the Romans

SECTION SIX:
What God Expects of Believers (12:1-15:13)

Using our Gifts and Talents (Romans 12:1-21)

(Read Romans 12:1,2)

[1] Brothers and sisters, God has shown you his mercy. So I am asking you to offer up your bodies to him while you are still alive. Your bodies are a holy sacrifice that is pleasing to God. When you offer your bodies to God, you are worshiping him. [2] Don't live any longer the way this world lives. Let your way of thinking be completely changed. Then you will be able to test what God wants for you. And you will agree that what he wants is right. His plan is good and pleasing and perfect.

In the previous chapter Paul explained the "mystery" of how God has shown mercy to both Jews and Gentiles. Now he tells them how to respond to God's mercy. He urges them to present themselves to God as living sacrifices.

In Old Testament times God commanded Israel to bring many sacrifices. Some of them were animal sacrifices. The animal was killed and presented to the Lord. These sacrifices taught the lesson that sinners deserve to die. They can be spared only by having a substitute die in their place. Such bloody sacrifices pointed ahead to Christ's sacrifice on the cross.

After Christ's death on the cross as our substitute, those bloody sacrifices are no longer necessary. But Paul suggests a new kind of sacrifice. It is not an animal offered as a substitute but the Christian offering himself to God. And he is not killed but presented as a living sacrifice. Being alive, this living sacrifice is able and eager to serve God.

We need to be very clear: this is not a service needed to make the believer acceptable to God. Christ has already done

Paul speaks to new believers.

that for us. What Paul is here talking about is the believer's thankful reaction to God's mercy.

Paul suggests two courses of action. The first is negative: "Don't live any longer the way this world lives." The second is positive: "Let your way of thinking be completely changed. Then you will be able to test what God wants for you."

The change in thinking Paul is speaking of happens when the Holy Spirit brings a person to faith. This change is often called "conversion." It gives the believer the "new man" who wants to do what pleases God. Paul describes such God-pleasing life in the next verses.

(Read Romans 12:3-8)

[3] God's grace has been given to me. So here is what I say to every one of you. Don't think of yourself more highly than you should. Be reasonable when you think about yourself. Keep in mind the amount of faith God has given you.
[4] Each of us has one body with many parts. And the parts do not all have the same purpose. [5] So also we are many persons. But in Christ we are one body. And each part of the body belongs to all the other parts.
[6] We all have gifts. They differ in keeping with the grace that God has given each of us. Do you have the gift of prophecy? Then use it in keeping with the faith you have. [7] Is it your gift to serve? Then serve. Is it teaching? Then teach. [8] Is it telling others how they should live? Then tell them. Is it giving to those who are in need? Then give freely. Is it being a leader? Then work hard at it. Is it showing mercy? Then do it cheerfully.

In describing the believer's new life that pleases God, Paul uses another negative and positive combination. First he says, "Don't think of yourself more highly than you should." Pride and arrogance are common problems. The proud person thinks he can do everything and he looks down on others less gifted. The apostle's advice is, "Be reasonable when you think about yourself."

But there is also an opposite problem. Some people think, "I can't do anything." Paul states positively, "We all have gifts." The situation is like what happens in the human body.

God gives us everything we need.

Different members do different things. Eyes, ears, nose, feet and hands are different, but they all work together to form one body.

The same is true in the Church, which is Christ's body. All believers have gifts, but "they differ in keeping with the grace God has given each of us." All believers with their various gifts join together to make Christ's Church work properly.

Paul lists seven examples of what Christians might do. He mentions prophesying (we could say "preaching"), serving, teaching, correcting others, charitable giving, leading, and showing mercy. These very general terms are just some suggestions. They are intended to make each of us ask ourselves, "What gifts has the Lord given me that I could use to please God and serve the people around me?"

Things to remember:

1. Paul asks believers to do what pleases God because God has shown them _____.
2. Paul urges believers to present themselves to God as living _____.
3. Paul urges: "Don't live any longer as the _____ lives."
4. Each of us has received _____ from God.
5. Believers use their gifts to _____ God and serve _____.

(Check your answers on page 153.)

Love Toward Everyone

(Read Romans 12:9-13)

⁹ Love must be honest and true. Hate what is evil. Hold on to what is good. ¹⁰ Love each other deeply. Honor others more than yourselves. ¹¹ Never let the fire in your heart go out. Keep it alive. Serve the Lord.

*Timothy is to remember what his mother
and grandmother taught him.*

[12] When you hope, be joyful. When you suffer, be patient. When you pray, be faithful. [13] Share with God's people who are in need. Welcome others into your homes.

The previous section made a number of suggestions on how to use our gifts in a Christian congregation. There are many different things thankful Christians can do for their fellow believers. The motivation for doing so, however, always remains the same. That motivation is love. Christian love for those around us moves us to serve them with the gifts God has given us.

In a paragraph that speaks so much about the necessity of love, it may seem strange to hear the apostle use the term "hate." But note what we are to hate. We are to hate evil. When Paul in the next sentence says, "Hold on to what is good," that is just another way of hating what is evil.

There is another feature of this section that calls attention to itself. It is all the short sentences Paul uses here. He apparently wants to make a number of suggestions, without going into great detail about any of them. It's like the bulleted items in an outline. Verses 12 and 13 serve as a good example:

- Be joyful.
- Be patient.
- Be faithful.
- Share with God's people.
- Welcome others.

The short sentences continue in the next verses, but notice that the circle of people to whom we are to show love becomes larger.

(Read Romans 12:14-16)

[14] Bless those who hurt you. Bless them, and do not call down curses on them. [15] Be joyful with those who are joyful. Be sad with those who are sad. [16] Agree with each other. Don't be proud. Be willing to be a friend of

people who aren't considered important. Don't think that you are better than others.

Paul continues to list various ways in which a child of God can show love to those around him. The number of suggestions he makes indicates that there are many ways in which this can be done.

The author continues to use short sentences to give additional encouragements, but there is also a significant difference. Previously Paul urged his readers to show love toward fellow believers. Now he widens the circle to include also non-Christians as objects of their love. He urges them, "Bless those who hurt you. Bless them, and do not call down curses on them."

Showing love toward fellow-believers whom we know and care about can often be challenging. But showing love toward those who hate and hurt us is even more difficult. In this part of his letter Paul has been using short sentences with very little explanation of the encouragements he is giving. Yet so important is the matter of Christians showing love toward non-Christians that he spends the next five verses urging such an attitude.

Things to remember:

6. First Paul urges his readers to show love toward
   _____ _____.

7. Then Paul widens the circle to include also
   _____.

8. Paul says, "Bless those who _____ you."
   (Check your answers on page 153.)

(Read Romans 12:17-21)

[17] Don't pay back evil with evil. Be careful to do what everyone thinks is right. [18] If possible, live in peace with everyone. Do that as much as you can.

[19] My friends, don't try to get even. Leave room for God to show his anger. It is written, "I am the One who judges people. I will pay them back,"—(*Deuteronomy 32:35*) says the Lord. [20] Do just the opposite. Scripture says,

"If your enemies are hungry, give them food to eat.

If they are thirsty, give them something to drink.

By doing those things, you will pile up burning coals on their heads."
—(*Proverbs 25:21,22*)

[21] Don't let evil overcome you. Overcome evil by doing good.

Paul writes, "If possible, live in peace with everyone. Do that as much as you can." Christians, reflecting Christ's love in their lives, will not be quarrelsome. They will not cause problems in the society where they live. But there will always be some people in society who promote ideas and actions that a child of God can not approve. Then it is necessary to resist such people and speak out against them.

Speaking out against their wrong thinking or their evil deeds will often cause confrontation and conflict. That may make it impossible for Christians to live at peace with some people. In fact, it is entirely possible that such confrontation may lead unbelieving opponents to harm Christians.

When it happens that Christians are harmed, Paul says, "Don't pay back evil with evil." But that is hard to do. Where will the child of God get the strength to resist paying back evil people?

Here we need to look to Christ's example. When the soldiers were nailing him to the cross, he prayed, "Father, forgive them; they don't know what they are doing."

But Christ is not just an example for us to follow. He is much more. He is also the One who gives us the strength to reflect his love by forgiving those who harm us. When we think of Christ's love for us and the sacrifice he made, then we too become willing to love and forgive those who sin against us.

There is also a second reason for Christians not to seek revenge. Paul says, "My friends don't try to get even. Leave room for God to show his anger." Christians do not have the task of correcting everything that is wrong in our society. God is in charge. If evil people insist on doing evil things, God does not forcibly stop them here on earth, but he does hold them accountable. Judgment day is coming. Then he will deal with them. Paul quotes the Old Testament book of Deuteronomy, where God says, "I am the One who judges people. I will pay them back."

Paul adds even a third reason for not seeking revenge. After saying, "Don't try to get even," he adds, "Do just the opposite." When your enemies mistreat you, treat them kindly. Then he adds some examples of how that can be done.

"If your enemies are hungry, give them food to eat.

If they are thirsty, give them something to drink."

Then Paul gives the reason for showing kind treatment to enemies. "By doing these things you will pile up burning coals on their heads." At first sight this could seem to be a way of getting back at our enemies. Paul obviously cannot mean that. Rather, he is using picture language to illustrate a feeling or a state of mind in the enemies. For them to receive kind treatment from people whom they have wronged can have the effect of giving them a very bad conscience. Their regret will be so intense that it feels like having fire on their heads.

The desired effect will be that the former enemies will see the error of their ways and will be drawn to Christ and his message of forgiveness. Although it will not always turn out favorably, winning over the enemy is the hoped-for outcome. In this way the Christian's "good" will have overcome the enemy's "evil." That is what Paul is urging when he says, "Don't let evil overcome you. Overcome evil by doing good."

Things to remember:

9. Don't pay back evil with _____.
10. If possible, live in _____ with everyone.
11. On judgment day _____ will punish evildoers.
12. Kind treatment to enemies is intended to win them for

_____.

(Check your answers on page 153.)

At the beginning of the previous chapter Paul reminded his readers that in Christ God has showed them great mercy. Because they have received God's mercy, the apostle urged them to present themselves to God as "living sacrifices." One way they can do this is by living lives that reflect Christ's love toward others. They are to do this, even to the extent of loving their enemies and trying to win them over.

In this next chapter Paul encourages his readers to show their appreciation for God's mercy by living lives of obedience to the rulers God has placed over them.

Obey Those in Authority (Romans 13:1-7)

(Read Romans 13:1,2)

[1] All of you must be willing to obey completely those who rule over you. There are no authorities except the ones God has chosen. Those who now rule have been chosen by God. [2] So when you oppose the authorities, you are opposing those whom God has appointed. Those who do that will be judged.

God is the Creator. He has made everything and everything belongs to him. He rules and directs all things in this world. However, God does not come directly and visibly into our lives. Rather, he rules through various authorities who represent him. Disobeying his representatives is like disobeying God himself.

God has put parents in charge of home and family. He calls workers into church service. In the workplace foremen and bosses are in charge. In various ways God places people into public service and government offices.

Paul states, "There are no authorities except the ones God has chosen. Those who now rule have been chosen by God." In writing to the Romans, Paul is no doubt thinking especially of the emperor and his imperial government in Rome. These authorities were pagan, not Christian. The emperor at this time most likely was the notorious Nero who persecuted Christians. Yet Paul urges his readers not to oppose the government. In fact, he warns, "Those who do that will be judged."

But it is not just a fear of punishment that should make people obey those in authority. Paul mentions another reason.

(Read Romans 13:3,4)

[3] If you do what is right, you won't need to be afraid of your rulers. But watch out if you do what is wrong! You don't want to be afraid of those in authority, do you? Then do what is right. The one in authority will praise you. [4] He serves God and will do you good. But if you do wrong, watch out! The ruler doesn't carry a sword for no reason at all. He serves God. And God is carrying out his anger through him. The ruler punishes anyone who does wrong.

"If you do what is right, you won't need to be afraid of your rulers…. [They] serve God and will do you good." With these words Paul gives another reason for co-operating with the authorities. They serve God and through them God wants to do us good.

We need to be reminded how great a blessing stable government is. Some times government does not properly represent God, but when it does, it brings great blessings. It allows us to live in a peaceful society without the fear of violence. It allows us to be employed at productive work and

Pontius Pilate presents Jesus to an angry crowd.

to enjoy our times of leisure. Most important of all, it allows us to worship in peace and to invite others to come and share in the blessings God has shown us.

God is a God of peace and order. Because these are such precious gifts, God guards them carefully. He directs his representatives (government) to administer punishment for wrong-doers who spoil those gifts for others.

At times a government's punishment can be severe. That is because "God is carrying out his anger through him." God is the giver of life. He is also the One who can take life. Through the actions of his representative (government) God may take the life of a serious offender. That is what Paul is referring to when he writes, "If you do wrong, watch out! The ruler doesn't carry a sword for no reason at all. He serves God." Scripture does not command the death penalty, but it does not forbid it either.

(Read Romans 13:5-7)

[5] You must obey the authorities. Then you will not be punished. You must also obey them because you know it is right.
[6] That's also why you pay taxes. The authorities serve God. Ruling takes up all their time. [7] Give to everyone what you owe. Do you owe taxes? Then pay them. Do you owe anything else to the government? Then pay it. Do you owe respect? Then give it. Do you owe honor? Then show it.

Paul adds yet another reason for obeying authorities. He says, "You must also obey them because you know it is right." It is right to obey because rulers are God's representatives. Obeying them is like obeying God himself. As creatures, we know that we ought to obey our Creator.

This realization helps us to do what we ought to do. Paying taxes is not something we would choose to do. However, realizing that through his representatives God is asking us to pay our taxes makes us willing to obey. We know it is the right thing to do.

Paying taxes is just one example of proper obedience. Paul broadens out his encouragement when he adds, "Do you owe anything else to the government? Then pay it."

Paying with money is an outward and external thing. Even more important than the outward action is the attitude of the heart. A Christian citizen will carry out his obligations cheerfully, showing honor and respect for the authorities. After all, they represent God himself.

Things to remember:

13. Rulers and authorities are placed over us by

_____.

14. Rulers are called by God to punish those who do

_____ and to reward those who do

_____.

15. When obeying rulers, the attitude of our _____ is just as important as the outward _____.

(Check your answers on page 153.)

Show Love Now Because Judgment Day is Coming (Romans 13:8-14)

(Read Romans 13:8-10)

[8] Pay everything you owe. But you can never pay back all the love you owe each other. Those who love others have done everything the law requires. [9] Here are some commandments to think about. "Do not commit adultery." "Do not commit murder." "Do not steal." "Do not want what belongs to others."—(*Exodus 20:13-15,17; Deuteronomy 5:17-19,21*) These and other commandments are all included in one rule. Here's what it is. "Love your neighbor as you love yourself."—(*Leviticus 19:18*) [10] Love does not harm its neighbor. So love does everything the law requires.

Paying our taxes or paying other bills usually involves definite numbers. We can pay the required amount and then say, "There! I'm done with that. I don't owe any more." Paul encourages such an approach when he says, "Pay everything you owe."

But there is one debt we will never get fully paid. We can never say to people around us, "There! I've loved you enough. I don't need to show any more love." Such an approach would be totally contrary to what God expects of people who want to keep his Commandments.

In the previous section dealing with obeying our rulers, Paul was referring to the Fourth Commandment. Here in verse 9 he adds the Sixth Commandment, the Fifth, the Seventh, and the Ninth and Tenth Commandments (in that order). As his quotation from the Old Testament book of Leviticus shows, all of these commands can be reduced to just one word: Love. "Love your neighbor as you love yourself."

Love is the central requirement in all the Commandments. The first three deal with love toward God. The remaining seven speak of love toward our neighbor. Love is commanded in each of them. Showing love is not something that can be put off. There is urgency about it. Judgment day is coming.

Things to remember:
16. The central requirement of all the Commandments is to

_____.

17. Showing love toward others is a debt we can never fully

_____.

18. It is urgent that we love our neighbors because

_____ _____ is coming.

(Check your answers on page 153.)

(Read Romans 13:11,12)

[11] When you do those things, keep in mind the times we are living in. The hour has come for you to wake up from your sleep. Our full salvation is closer now than it was when we first believed in Christ. [12] The dark

night of evil is nearly over. The day of Christ's return is almost here. So let us get rid of the works of darkness. Let us put on the armor of light.

Christians at every stage of history have always known they were living in "end times." Our time on earth is limited. It will end either with our physical death or the Lord's coming to judge.

Here in Romans the apostle's time reference is to judgment day. He says, "The day of Christ's return is almost here." The passing of every 24 hours brings Christ's return one day closer. Note the positive turn the apostle gives this when he says, "Our full salvation is closer now than it was when we first believed in Christ." Already here on earth the believer is saved but the full realization of that salvation will not come until we are taken to heaven.

By reminding us of Christ's return to judge the world Paul is not trying to scare us. Rather, he is pointing out that our time here on earth is short. We need to be busy and active in living the life of love needed to fulfill the Commandments. He urges both a negative and a positive approach in our life. Negatively he says, "So let us get rid of the works of darkness." Positively he says, "Let us put on the armor of light."

(Read Romans 13:13,14)

[13] Let us act as we should, like people living in the daytime. Have nothing to do with wild parties. Don't get drunk. Don't take part in sexual sins or evil conduct. Don't fight with each other. Don't be jealous of anyone.
[14] Instead, put on the Lord Jesus Christ as your clothing. Don't think about how to satisfy what your sinful nature wants.

Paul has urged his readers to get rid of the works of darkness. Without going into detail he now gives some examples of things to avoid. He puts them into short sentences that easily form a list:

- Have nothing to do with wild parties.
- Don't get drunk.
- Don't take part in sexual sins or evil conduct.
- Don't fight with each other.
- Don't be jealous of anyone.

These are only some examples. The apostle is urging each of us to make our own list of pet sins and temptations to avoid. With judgment day coming, this is no time to be spiritually asleep. Paul gives needed encouragement when he says, "Let us act as we should, like people living in the daytime."

But where can we go to find the strength to resist temptation? How will we get rid of the works of darkness? Paul answers, "Let us put on the armor of light." Putting on the armor of light is picture language for putting on protection against the works of darkness.

In verse 14 the apostle explains more fully what Christians are to put on. He changes the picture a bit when he says, "Put on the Lord Jesus as your clothing." In his letter to the Galatians Paul explains even more clearly what this means. There he says, "You are all children of God by believing in Christ Jesus. All of you who were baptized into Christ have put on Christ as if he were your clothes" (Galatians 3:26,27).

Christ's perfect life and innocent death paid for all the sins and wickedness we sinners have ever done. Through baptism, which worked faith in our hearts, Christ's righteousness was put over us like a garment. It covers our ugly sin. God can now look at us and see us as holy because we are clothed with Christ's righteousness.

But putting on the Lord Jesus Christ not only makes us acceptable to God. It also gives us the strength to do the things that please God. Baptized into Christ and clothed with his righteousness, we have a "new man" who fights against our "old Adam." Putting on Christ enables the new man to put off the works of darkness. Now, instead of doing bad things, the new man in us can begin to show the loving service to God and our neighbor that the Commandments call for.

Things to remember:
19. Paul warns us to avoid "works of _____."
20. Putting on the armor of light means putting on _____ against the works of darkness.
21. Putting on the Lord Jesus as clothing means accepting his _____ as a cover for our _____.
22. Believers have a _____ _____ who is able to _____ as the Commandments require.

(Check your answers on page 153.)

The central theme of Paul's letter to the Romans is: Righteous through faith. That refers first of all to the righteousness of Christ that becomes ours simply by believing it. But there is also another kind of righteousness. That is the righteousness that the believer is able to show in his own life and actions. We have already seen two examples of such righteousness. In chapter 12 the apostle urged us to use our God-given gifts in loving service of others. Chapter 13 urged us to obey the authorities God has put over us as his representatives. Now in chapters 14 and 15 Paul adds a third area. That area involves strong believers being kind and considerate toward spiritually weak brothers and sisters.

Strong and Weak Believers (Romans 14:1 – 15:13)
Opinions Concerning Food

(Read Romans 14:1-4)

[1] Accept those whose faith is weak. Don't judge them where you have differences of opinion.

[2] The faith of some people allows them to eat anything. But others eat only vegetables because their faith is weak. [3] People who eat everything must not look down on those who do not. And people who don't eat everything must not judge those who do. God has accepted them.

[4] Who are you to judge someone else's servants? Whether they are faithful or not is their own master's concern. They will be faithful, because the Lord has the power to make them faithful.

Not everyone has the same degree of spiritual understanding. Some are mature Christians who have been believers for a long time. Others are new to the faith and still have many things to learn from their study of Scripture. Weak faith is saving faith, but strong believers are to help the weaker ones grow.

It is to the more mature Christians among his readers that Paul says, "Accept those whose faith is weak. Don't judge them where you have differences of opinion."

It is important to know what things the strong are to tolerate and accept. Paul is here NOT talking about doctrine. Paul is not saying, "Don't worry about it if someone teaches false doctrine." In chapter 16 he will warn his readers to stay away from false teachers. What the strong brothers are to accept and not judge are differences of opinion. He is referring to thoughts and actions that are neutral. These are things where one person may have one opinion and his neighbor holds a different opinion. Neither opinion is sinful. Paul gives an example. Some people eat one kind of food, others eat something else. Neither choice is bad.

Paul is writing to a mixed congregation. Most were Gentiles. Some were Jews. Remember that in the Old Testament God chose the Jews as his special people. From them the Savior of the world would be born. To keep the Jewish people separate from other nations, God gave them special rules. Among those special rules were instructions as to what foods they could eat. Some were "clean" foods. These they could eat. Others, like pork, were "unclean." Jews were forbidden to eat such foods.

These special rules were to keep the Jewish nation separate until the promised Savior was born from them. After Christ's coming there was no longer any need to have special food rules. But some Jewish Christians had misgivings about eating what for centuries they had considered unclean. It bothered them that the Gentiles, who had never had those special rules, ate anything and everything on the menu. In this specific instance the Gentiles were ahead of the Jews in practicing their Christian liberty.

To these "stronger" Gentile believers among his readers Paul gives the advice, "People who eat everything must not look down on those who do not." And to the "weaker" Jewish readers he says, "And people who don't eat everything must not judge those who do."

The basis for Paul's advice is, "God has accepted [both of] them." God doesn't care what anyone eats. That is an individual choice every person is free to make. God is satisfied either way. Paul illustrates the believer's relationship to God by comparing it to that of a master and his servant. If the master is satisfied with what his servant is doing, "Who are you to judge someone else's servant?"

There are many situations in life where God's Word does not decide for us what we should do. Then we are free to have our own opinion. Paul's concern is that we do not make a problem by insisting on having our way in a neutral matter. When there is a difference of opinion among Christians, the strong will be considerate of their weaker brothers and sisters. In this way there will be peace and harmony.

That lesson in Christian living, however, is not easily learned. Paul stresses the importance of this matter by bringing another example of the strong needing to be considerate of their weaker brothers and sisters. This time he speaks of choosing a day for worship.

Things to remember:

23. For many centuries the _____ lived under special rules to keep them separate from other nations.
24. These special rules pointed ahead to _____.
25. After Christ came it was no longer necessary to

    _____.

26. It took a while for some New Testament Christians to realize they didn't need to keep these special rules. While they are learning Paul asks the _____ members to be considerate of the _____ members.

(Check your answers on page 153.)

(Read Romans 14:5-6)

[5] Some people consider one day to be more holy than another. Others think all days are the same. Each person should be absolutely sure in his own mind. [6] Those who think one day is special do it to honor the Lord. Those who eat meat do it to honor the Lord. They give thanks to God. Those who don't eat meat do it to honor the Lord. They also give thanks to God.

Remember that Paul is writing to a mixed group of Jewish and Gentile believers. With this example Paul seems to be referring to another neutral area or opinion that needed to be dealt with tactfully in order to unite this group.

Throughout the centuries of the Old Testament the Jewish nation had, by God's command, observed the Sabbath (Saturday) as a day of rest. The Sabbath regulations were a teaching device. They pointed forward to the rest for their souls that Jesus would bring them. After Christ came and brought the promised rest through his saving work, it was no longer necessary to observe the Sabbath rules and to worship on Saturday. The New Testament Christian church was free to choose its own day. In Christian liberty they chose Sunday as their day of worship.

There no doubt was a group in Rome that felt they should keep Saturday as their worship day. Others felt free to change to another day. Paul describes the situation with the words, "Some people consider one day to be more holy than another. Others think all days are the same." Of those who wanted to keep the Sabbath Paul says, "Those who think one day is special do it to honor the Lord." But the same was true of the group that wanted to worship on Sunday. They too were doing it to honor their Lord, who rose on Easter Sunday.

Both groups in Rome wanted to honor the Lord. Neither side was doing anything wrong. It was another case of where the situation needed to be resolved by the strong being considerate of their weaker brothers and sisters.

In the first example of weak brothers being unclear regarding the freedom to eat all kinds of food, Paul made the point, "God has accepted them." They are his servants. Who are you to judge them if God has accepted them? Here in this second example Paul brings a different reason for showing kind treatment to weak brothers. Here he states that all of us, strong and weak, live our lives under the same circumstances. We live together; we die together; we will all be judged together.

Things to remember:

27. In the Old Testament the Jews were commanded by God to worship on _____.

28. New Testament Christians may worship on

_____ _____.

(Check your answers on page 153.)

(Read Romans 14:7-12)

[7] We don't live for ourselves alone. And we don't die all by ourselves. [8] If we live, we live to honor the Lord. If we die, we die to honor the Lord. So whether we live or die, we belong to the Lord.

[9] Christ died and came back to life. He did this to become the Lord of

both the dead and the living.

[10] Now then, who are you to judge your brother or sister? Why do you look down on them? We will all stand in God's courtroom to be judged. It is written, " 'You can be sure that I live,' says the Lord.

'And you can be just as sure that every knee will bow down in front of me.

Every tongue will tell the truth to God.' "—(*Isaiah 45:23*) [12] So we will all have to explain to God the things we have done.

It is important to remember that Paul is here speaking of Christians who are dealing with fellow-Christians. They are brothers and sisters in the faith. They have a common goal. Everything they are doing in faith is being done to honor the Lord.

Speaking to the strong Christians Paul says, "Now then, who are you to judge your brother or sister? Why do you look down on them? We will all stand in God's courtroom to be judged."

Paul points out that death is the great equalizer. It brings all people to the same place. That place is God's courtroom on judgment day. There, the prophet Isaiah says, "Every tongue will tell the truth to God." Paul adds his own comment, "So we will all have to explain to God the things we have done." There is one great transgression no one will want to confess on that day. That is the sin of having destroyed a weak brother's faith so that he has lost his salvation. Paul warns against that dread possibility in the next section.

(Read Romans 14.13-23)

[13] Let us stop judging one another. Instead, make up your mind not to put anything in your brother's way that would make him trip and fall.

[14] I am absolutely sure that no food is "unclean" in itself. I say this as one who belongs to the Lord Jesus. But some people may consider a thing to be "unclean." If they do, it is "unclean" for them. [15] Your brothers and sisters may be upset by what you eat. If they are, you are no longer acting as though you love them. So don't destroy them by what you eat. Christ

died for them. [16] Don't let something you consider good be spoken of as if it were evil.

[17] God's kingdom has nothing to do with eating or drinking. It is a matter of being right with God. It brings the peace and joy the Holy Spirit gives.

[18] Those who serve Christ in this way are pleasing to God. They are pleasing to people too.

[19] So let us do all we can to live in peace. And let us work hard to build each other up.

[20] Don't destroy the work of God because of food. All food is "clean." But it is wrong for you to eat anything that causes someone else to trip and fall. [21] Don't eat meat if it will cause your brothers and sisters to fall. Don't drink wine or do anything else that will make them fall.

[22] No matter what you think about those things, keep it between yourself and God. Blessed are those who do not have to feel guilty for what they allow.

[23] But those who have doubts are guilty if they eat. Their eating is not based on faith. Everything that is not based on faith is sin.

Speaking to the strong Christians Paul says, "Let us stop judging one another. Instead, make up your mind not to put anything in your brother's way that would make him trip and fall." When the apostle speaks of someone tripping and falling he means that in a spiritual sense. As he will explain below, he is describing a weak believer falling from faith and losing his salvation.

To show how this can happen he returns to the previous illustration of clean and unclean foods. It may be easier to follow Paul's thinking here if we group similar sentences together.

In verse 17 Paul makes the general statement, "God's kingdom has nothing to do with eating or drinking. It is a matter of being right with God." Accepting Christ's righteousness by faith is all that is necessary. There is no need to be eating the right things in order to be saved. That thought fits with verse 14a, where he earlier said, "I am absolutely sure that no food is 'unclean' in itself. I say this as one who belongs to the Lord Jesus."

Verse 14b however calls attention to a possible problem: "But some people may consider a thing to be 'unclean.' If they do, it is 'unclean' for them." Paul says there actually are no unclean foods. A weak brother may mistakenly think that a food item is unclean. He thinks God has forbidden him to eat it—but he goes ahead and eats it anyway. He is basically rebelling against God. He is denying his faith and in danger of losing his salvation. Paul explains that more fully in verse 23, "Those who have doubts are guilty if they eat. Their eating is not based on faith. Everything that is not based on faith is sin."

The strong brother may become involved if he eats what the weak brother considers unclean food. The weak brother has a bad conscience for doing it, but he follows the strong brother's example and also eats the food in question. Paul pictures such a situation in verse 15, "Your brothers and sisters may be upset by what you eat. If they are, you are no longer acting as though you love them. So don't destroy them by what you eat. Christ died for them,"

That the weak brother has been brought to faith is clearly God's work. That is why Paul is so determined in warning strong Christians in verses 20 and 21, "Don't destroy the work of God because of food. All food is 'clean.' But it is wrong for you to eat anything that causes someone else to trip and fall. Do not eat meat if it will cause your brothers and sisters to fall. Do not drink wine or do anything else that will make them fall."

The proper thing to do, of course, is for the strong brothers lovingly and patiently to teach the weaker members of the congregation. Paul urges them in verse 19, "So let us do all we can to live in peace. And let us work hard to build each other up." Building up weaker brothers includes teaching them the full scope of their Christian liberty. Until the weak have reached that level of maturity, the strong brothers will best serve the situation by giving up their right to eat and drink whatever they please. Such patient instruction "brings the peace and joy the Holy Spirit gives" (v. 17b).

Things to Remember:

29. Paul warns strong Christians not to do anything that would harm the _____ of a weaker brother.

30. If a weak Christian does what is not wrong, but he thinks that it is wrong, he is committing a _____. He is rebelling against _____.

31. Strong brothers need to be careful that their example does not lead weaker Christians to do what they think is _____.

(Check your answers on page 153.)

(Read Romans 15:1-6)

[1] We who have strong faith should help the weak with their problems. We should not please only ourselves. [2] We should all please our neighbors. Let us do what is good for them. Let us build them up.

[3] Even Christ did not please himself. It is written, "Those who make fun of you have made fun of me also."—(*Psalm 69:9*) [4] Everything that was written in the past was written to teach us. The Scriptures give us strength to go on. They cheer us up and give us hope.

[5] Our God is a God who strengthens you and cheers you up. May he help you agree with each other as you follow Christ Jesus. [6] Then you can give glory to God with one heart and voice. He is the God and Father of our Lord Jesus Christ.

Speaking to the strong members of the congregation in Rome Paul urges them to deal patiently with their weaker brothers. He says, "Let us do what is good for them. Let us build them up."

But showing such unselfish service to others is a very difficult assignment. Where are they to get the strength to do this properly? Paul draws their attention, first of all, to the

Jesus promises the Holy Spirit to teach his disciples.

example of their Savior. He tells them, "Even Christ did not please himself."

But Christ is more than just an example for us to follow using our own will power. Christ also gives us the ability to do what is needed. The apostle assures his readers, "Our God is a God who strengthens you and cheers you up." God does that strengthening through his Word. Paul says. "Everything that was written in the past was written to teach us. The Scriptures give us strength to go on."

Christians drawing strength from Scripture is something that goes on every day. It is happening right now as we study Paul's letter to the Romans. We are strengthened by the apostle's inspired words. Also, it is reassuring to realize that as readers of his letter we too are included in his prayer, "May [God] help you agree with each other as you follow Christ Jesus. Then you can give glory to God with one heart and voice."

Things to remember:

32. Christians can find an example of how to treat others by looking at _____.
33. To gain the strength needed to follow Christ's example we need to read and study the _____.
(Check your answers on page 153.)

(Read Romans 15:7-13)

[7] Christ has accepted you. So accept one another in order to bring praise to God.

[8] I tell you that Christ has become a servant of the Jews. He teaches us that God is true. He shows us that God will keep the promises he made to the founders of our nation. [9] Jesus became a servant of the Jews so that people who are not Jews could give glory to God for his mercy. It is written,

"I will praise you among those who aren't Jews.

I will sing praises to you."—(2 Samuel 22:50; Psalm 18:49)
[10] Again it says,

"You non-Jews, be full of joy.
    Be joyful together with God's people."—(*Deuteronomy 32:43*)
[11] And again it says,
"All you non-Jews, praise the Lord.
    All you nations, sing praises to him."—(*Psalm 117:1*) [12] And Isaiah says,
"The Root of Jesse will grow up quickly.
    He will rule over the nations.
    Those who aren't Jews will put their hope in him."—(*Isaiah 11:10*)
[13] May the God who gives hope fill you with great joy. May you have perfect peace as you trust in him. May the power of the Holy Spirit fill you with hope.

When Paul writes, "Christ has accepted you" he is talking to both groups in Rome, the strong and the weak. They have cultural differences, but he urges them to get along peacefully "in order to bring praise to God." It is reasonable for Paul to assume they can do this because they have a great blessing in common. Christ has accepted them. Christ has become a "servant" to both groups.

First the author reminds them of God's faithfulness in dealing with the Jewish nation. "I tell you that Christ has become a servant of the Jews. He (Christ) teaches us that God is true. He shows us that God will keep the promises he made to the founders of our nation."

God's sending Christ into the world shows that God can be trusted to keep his promises. Many, many years earlier God had promised Abraham that he and his wife Sarah would have a son. This son would become the father of a great nation. From that nation the Savior promised already to Adam and Eve in the Garden of Eden would come. All of these things had happened when Paul was writing to the church in Rome. His Jewish readers can be sure that also in the future "God will keep the promises he made to the founders of our nation."

But Christ is a servant not only to the Jewish nation. God clearly stated that the Savior to come from Abraham's descendants was to be a blessing to all nations. This too was fulfilled in the person of Jesus of Nazareth. Paul calls this to his readers' attention when he writes, "Jesus became a servant of the Jews so that people who are not Jews could give glory to God for his mercy."

Remember that in the middle part of this letter Paul devoted three chapters (9-11) to show how God had shown mercy to the Gentiles. When most of the Jews rejected the message of salvation through faith in Christ Jesus, God took that saving message and gave it to the Gentiles.

Paul's mission work among the Gentiles was a very clear example of this major turn of events. But even though taking the gospel to the Gentiles was a later event in history, it was not an afterthought on God's part. Including Gentiles was not Plan B, as though Plan A with the Jewish nation had failed. God's saving plan always included the Gentiles. Paul emphasizes this important truth by quoting four Old Testament prophecies that speak of "non-Jews" receiving God's mercy.

It is written,
"I will praise you among **those who aren't Jews**.
   I will sing praises to you."—(*2 Samuel 22:50; Psalm 18:49*)
 Again it says,
 "You **non-Jews**, be full of joy.
   Be joyful together with God's people."—(*Deuteronomy 32:43*)
And again it says,
"All you **non-Jews**, praise the Lord.
   All you nations, sing praises to him."—(*Psalm 117:1*)
And Isaiah says,
"The Root of Jesse will grow up quickly.
   He will rule over the nations.
   Those who **aren't Jews** will put their hope in him."—(*Isaiah 11:10*)

Things to remember:

34. Christ became a _____ to both Jews
    and Gentiles.
35. Saving Gentiles was not an idea that began in the New
    Testament. It was foretold already by the _____

    _____ _____.

(Check your answers on page 153.)

Paul closes this section on uniting strong and weak
brothers by praying for them. It is a prayer he started back in
verses 5 and 6. Here in verse 13 he finishes that prayer with
the words, "May the God who gives hope fill you with great
joy. May you have perfect peace as you trust in him. May the
power of the Holy Spirit fill you with hope." It is a prayer
that fits our situation also.

Things to remember-Answers

1. mercy; 2. sacrifices; 3. world; 4. gifts; 5. please, others; 6. fellow
Christians; 7. non-Christians; 8. hate; 9. evil; 10. peace; 11. God;
12. Christ; 13. God; 14. evil, good; 15. heart, actions; 16. love; 17. pay;
18. judgment day; 19. darkness; 20. protection; 21. righteousness, sins;
22. new man, live; 23. Jews; 24. Christ; 25. keep special rules; 26. strong,
weak; 27. Saturday; 28. any day; 29. faith; 30. sin, God; 31. wrong;
32. Jesus; 33. Bible; 34. servant; 35. Old Testament prophets.

TEST - Righteous Through Faith:
A Study of the Epistle to the Romans

Section 6
Please review the "Things to remember."

1. Paul asks believers to do what pleases God because God has shown them _____.

2. Paul urges believers to present themselves to God as living _____.

3. Each of us has received _____ from God. Believers use their gifts to _____ God and to serve _____.

4. First Paul urges his readers to show love toward _____. Then he widens the circle to include also _____.

5. Don't pay back evil with _____. If possible, live in _____ with everyone.

6. Rulers and authorities are placed over us by _____. Rulers are called to punish those who do _____ and to reward those who do _____.

7. When obeying rulers, the attitude of our _____ is just as important as our outward _____.

8. The central requirement of all the Commandments is to _____.

9. In the Old Testament the Jews were commanded by God to worship on _____. New Testament Christians may worship on _____ _____.

10. Paul warns strong Christians not to do anything that would harm the _____ of a weaker brother.

11. If a weak Christian does what is not wrong, but he thinks that it is wrong, he is committing a _____. He is rebelling against _____.

12. Strong brothers need to be careful that their example does not lead weaker Christians to do what they think is _____.

13. Christians can find an example of how to treat others by looking at _____.

14. To gain the strength needed to follow Christ's example we need to read and study the _____.

15. Christ became a _____ to both Jews and Gentiles.

16. Saving Gentiles was not an idea that began in the New Testament. It was foretold already by the _____ _____ _____ _____.

(Check your answers on page 193.)

RIGHTEOUS
THROUGH FAITH

Righteous Through Faith:
A Study of the Epistle to the Romans

SECTION SEVEN:
Paul's Personal Plans (Romans 15:14-33)

Paul's Approach to Mission Work
Outreach to Gentiles

(Read Romans 15:14-16)

[14] My brothers and sisters, I am sure that you are full of goodness. What you know is complete. You are able to teach one another.
[15] I have written to you very boldly about some things. I wanted you to think about them again. The grace of God has allowed me [16] to serve Christ Jesus among those who aren't Jews. My duty as a priest is to preach God's good news. Then the non-Jews will become an offering that pleases God. The Holy Spirit will make the offering holy.

Remember that in the opening chapter of Romans Paul said that he has not been to Rome. Therefore, Paul did not start the church in Rome. They are Christian because of someone else's work. Note how generous the apostle is in judging their training and Christian maturity: They are full of goodness. Their knowledge is complete. They are able to teach others.

It is this maturity that allows Paul to speak very plainly to them. "I have written to you very boldly about some things." He does not tell us what those things are, but the next sentence shows clearly what he is talking about. "The grace of God has allowed me to serve Christ Jesus among those who aren't Jews."

The boldest thing Paul did was to take the message of Jesus of Nazareth, a Jewish Messiah, and proclaim it to the Gentiles. That was the cause of the bitter opposition the apostle received at the hands of his Jewish countrymen. Paul

God cares for Paul and Silas in prison in Philippi.

always started his outreach work at the local synagogue. When the local Jews refused to accept his message, Paul regularly declared, as he did in Antioch, "We had to speak the word of God to you first. Since you reject it and do not consider yourselves worthy of eternal life, we now turn to the Gentiles" (Acts 13;46). Going to the Gentiles brought fierce opposition against Paul and his coworkers, leading to beatings and even stoning.

Paul compares his work with Gentiles to that of an Old Testament priest. A priest was a "middle man" who took the worshiper's offering and presented it to the Lord. Paul views himself as such a "middle man" when he says, "My duty as a priest is to preach God's good news. Then the non-Jews will become an offering that pleases God. The Holy Spirit will make the offering holy."

Things to remember:
1. A priest's duty was to bring _____ to God.
2. The offering Paul as a priest brings to God is

_____ _____.

(Check your answers on page 169.)

(Read Romans 15:17-19)

[17] Because I belong to Christ Jesus, I can take pride in my work for God.
[18] I will not try to speak of anything except what Christ has done through me. He has been leading those who aren't Jews to obey God. He has been doing this by what I have said and done.
[19] He has given me power to do signs and miracles. He has given me the power of the Holy Spirit.

Paul's work among the Gentiles was very controversial, but he is by no means defensive or apologetic about it. Far from it. Without any hesitation he says, "Because I belong to Christ Jesus, I can take pride in my work for God."

Paul could have boasted. He was a powerful preacher

who could rightly claim that many conversions came about "by what I have said and done." God had given him the power to do signs and wonders. He could even say God had given him "the power of the Holy Spirit."

Paul could have boasted, but he doesn't. Rather he says, "I will not try to speak of anything except what Christ has done through me."

Outreach to New Territories

(Read Romans 15:19b-22)

From Jerusalem all the way around to Illyricum I have finished preaching the good news about Christ. [20] I have always wanted to preach the good news where Christ was not known. I don't want to build on what someone else has started. [21] It is written,

"Those who were not told about him will understand.

Those who have not heard will know what it all means."—(*Isaiah 52:15*) [22] That's why I have often been kept from coming to you.

In the paragraph just finished we noted one feature of Paul's ministry. He has a specific audience to which he wants to preach the gospel. He is an apostle to the Gentiles. In this next reading we note another aspect of his outreach method. His ministry has a territorial restriction. Paul does not go to places where other Christian missionaries have worked before him. He says "I have always wanted to preach the good news where Christ was not known. I don't want to build on what someone else has started." That approach agrees with what the prophet Isaiah foretold when he wrote, "Those who were not told about him (Christ) will understand. Those who have not heard will know what it all means."

This does not mean that Paul went wherever he chose. In Acts 16:6,7 we are told that God prevented him from preaching in the province of Asia Minor. Instead God in a vision called him to Macedonia in Europe. Obedient to God's direction, Paul preached in the regions along the northeastern seaboard of the Mediterranean Following that pattern for a number of years allows him now to say, "From Jerusalem all the way around to Illyricum I have finished preaching the good news about Christ."

The New Testament Christian church began in Jerusalem on Pentecost. From there the church spread to the countryside of Judea and then out into the non-Jewish world. Jerusalem was the starting point. The other end of the arc Paul refers to is the Roman province of Illyricum, lying just east of Italy. It would be the modern country of Albania and its neighbors that formerly were known as Yugoslavia.

Regarding the territory lying between Jerusalem and Illyricum Paul can say, "I have finished preaching the good news about Christ." We should not think that no more gospel preaching was now necessary in these territories. He is not saying that he had personally approached every individual with the gospel. Nor has he been in every town and village.

To understand the situation correctly we need to note another aspect of Paul's mission method. He went to major population centers in the various territories, such as the large city of Ephesus in Asia Minor and Corinth in Greece. After he established a congregation in an urban setting, Paul moved on to the next area. Meanwhile his co-worker and fellow missionaries stayed behind to continue working in the area. They served the established congregation and used it as a base for carrying the gospel message out to the surrounding countryside with its towns and villages.

Paul is not complaining about the special conditions God has attached to his mission ministry. Rather, he is explaining why it has taken him so long to visit them in Rome. There have been places not served by others where he needed to preach the gospel. These were the urban centers in the eastern Mediterranean countries to which God directed him. They have taken priority. But now that he has "finished preaching

Paul prays with the elders at Ephesus.

the good news about Christ" in these regions, he is free to come to Rome.

Things to remember:

3. Paul did not try to establish congregations in areas where others had _____.

4. Paul founded congregations in _____ areas. After he moved on to other places, his co-workers took the gospel out to the _____

_____.

5. Using this method of preaching in urban centers, Paul finished preaching the gospel from _____ to _____.

(Check your answers on page 169.)

(Read Romans 15:23,24)

[23] Now there is no more place for me to work in those areas. For many years I have been longing to see you. [24] So I plan to see you when I go to Spain. I hope to visit you while I am passing through. And I hope you will help me on my journey there. But first I want to enjoy being with you for a while.

Paul says, "For many years I have been longing to see you." That allows us to conclude that there has been a Christian congregation in Rome for some years already. Paul did not found the congregation. But we do not know who did. Acts 2:10 tells us that at Pentecost when the Holy Spirit was poured out on the apostles "visitors from Rome" were in attendance. Perhaps they went home and shared the message. Also, there was a saying in ancient times. "All roads lead to Rome." Perhaps Christians from the eastern Mediterranean areas moved to Rome and formed a Christian group there. We don't know.

One of the limitations of Paul's ministry was that he did not build on other people's work. He did not start congregations where others had already shared the gospel. Notice Paul's careful choice of words here. He does not say that he is coming to bring them the gospel. Rather he says, "I have been longing to see you...I hope to visit you....I want to enjoy being with you for a while." Paul is coming to them simply as a fellow Christian. He wants to enjoy their company for a while.

Christian fellowship, being together with other believers, is a great joy and a precious blessing. We need to take every opportunity we can to worship together, to receive the Lord's Supper together, to rejoice with each other in happy times and to comfort one another in times of trouble or sorrow. Even the great apostle Paul valued the company of "ordinary" fellow believers. We will want to do the same.

But in addition to an enjoyable visit there was yet another reason for Paul to write this letter to the Romans. Paul's outreach work in the eastern Mediterranean regions was finished. Now he could think of going to a new area—to the western Mediterranean region. He shares his plans when he tells the Romans, "So I plan to see you when I go to Spain. I hope to visit you while I am passing through. And I hope you will help me on my journey there."

Paul is likely thinking of going to Spain by ship. There were no passenger boats in early times. Travelers took passage on freighters and lived on the deck. They had to furnish their own food and provide protection against the elements. This, in addition to paying the fare for passage, involved considerable expense. In asking to be "helped on [his] journey" the apostle is suggesting that the Romans might like to pay for some of his travel costs.

Also, after arriving in Spain, Paul would need some money for daily living expenses. Here too the Romans could be helpful with a gift of money. Paul is giving his readers the chance to take part in a new mission venture in territory that had not yet heard the gospel message. However, before Paul can come to Rome and use their congregation as his starting place for outreach to Spain, there is one unfinished task he has to take care of.

Things to remember:

6. Paul shares his plan to go to the country of

    _____.

7. On his way to Spain he wants to

    _____ _____.

8. Paul invites the Romans to

    _____.

(Check your answers on page 169.)

(Read Romans 15:25-29)

[25] Now I am on my way to Jerusalem to serve God's people there. [26] The believers in Macedonia and Achaia (Greece) were pleased to take an offering for those who were poor among God's people in Jerusalem. [27] They were happy to do it. And of course they owe it to them. Those who aren't Jews have shared from the Jews' spiritual blessings. So the non-Jews should share their earthly blessings with the Jews.
[28] I want to finish my task. I want to make sure that the poor in Jerusalem have received the offering. Then I will go to Spain. On my way I will visit you. [29] I know that when I come to you, I will come with the full blessing of Christ.

Remember how much space Paul has devoted in this letter to the matter of Jewish and Gentile Christians getting along with each other. The apostle regularly urged strong brothers to help those who were weaker.

The poverty of many Jewish Christians in Jerusalem offered their Gentile brothers in Asia Minor and Europe an excellent opportunity to show their loving concern for these fellow believers. Under Paul's leadership the Gentile congregations took up a money collection. At the time of his writing to the Romans the money had been collected. Paul and a committee made up of members of the various contributing congregations were about to deliver this gift to Jerusalem. Paul is careful to do everything right. The gift is not only providing relief for physical needs. It also has spiritual implications. It is an indication of the unity that binds together fellow believers in Christ. When the important task of delivering the gift has been taken care of, then Paul can travel west to Rome and from there go on to Spain.

Incidentally, this is the only mention of Paul going to Spain. We do not know if he ever got there. The Bible is silent on that detail. Scripture tells us all that we need to know for salvation. It does not always answer things we might like to have more information about.

Things to remember:

9. Before going to Spain Paul had to deliver a
   _____ to _____.

10. The collection had two purposes. One was to provide
    _____ for the poor in Jerusalem.

11. A second purpose was to unify _____
    and _____.

(Check your answers on page 169.)

(Read Romans 15:30-33)

[30] Brothers and sisters, I am asking you through the authority of our Lord Jesus Christ to join me in my struggle by praying to God for me. Pray for me with the love the Holy Spirit provides. [31] Pray that I will be saved from those in Judea who do not believe. Pray that my work in Jerusalem will be accepted by God's people there. [32] Then, as God has planned, I will come to you with joy. Together we will be renewed.
[33] May the God who gives peace be with you all. Amen.

In verse 13 of this chapter Paul prayed for his Roman readers. In this paragraph he now asks the Romans to pray for him. There are basically two petitions.

On the one hand he makes the request, "Pray that my work in Jerusalem will be accepted by God's people there."

This is the spiritual aspect of the gift they are delivering. Paul is asking the Romans to pray for the result that Jews and Gentiles will be drawn closer together by this act of kindness. Achieving such an effect is not automatic. After all, Jews and Gentiles have been hostile and suspicious of each other for centuries. There is, however, good reason to hope that the desired effect will be accomplished here because this gift is going to "God's people" in Jerusalem.

The chances are not so good that Paul will be cordially received by the majority of the Jewish people who have rejected Christ and his message. Thinking of their opposition, Paul makes a second request, "Pray that I will be saved from those in Judea who do not believe."

Paul's fears were well-founded. When he arrived in Jerusalem he was mistakenly suspected of making the Temple unclean by bringing Gentiles into it. A mob assembled and a riot resulted. Paul was saved for the moment by Roman soldiers stationed in Jerusalem, but there was a bad side effect. Paul fell into the corrupt provincial legal system. To get justice he had to plead his case before Caesar in Rome. So, Paul did indeed get to Rome, but not in the way he planned. All of this, of course, is still in the future as Paul is writing this letter. Here he says in confident faith, "As God has planned, I will come to you with joy. Together we will be renewed."

Things to remember:

12. Paul asks the Romans to _____ for him.
13. Paul asks them to pray that the collection will be
    properly accepted by _____.
14. Paul asks them to pray that he will be protected against

    _____.

(Check your answers on page 169.)

Things to remember-Answers

1. offerings; 2. Gentile Christians; 3. worked before him; 4. urban, surrounding countryside; 5. Jerusalem, Illyricum; 6. Spain; 7. visit the Romans; 8. support his mission work in Spain; 9. collection, poor Christians in Jerusalem; 10. relief; 11. Jews, Gentiles; 12. pray; 13. Jewish Christians in Jerusalem; 14. unbelieving Jews in Jerusalem.

**TEST - Righteous Through Faith:
A Study of the Epistle to the Romans**

Section 7

Please review the "Things to remember."

1. A priest's duty was to bring _____ to God.

2. The offering Paul as a priest brings to God is

   _____ _____ .

3. Paul founded congregations in _____ areas.
   After he moved on to other places, his co-workers took
   the gospel out to _____ .

4. Paul shares his plan to go to the country of

   _____ .

5. On his way to Spain he wants to _____ .

6. Paul invites the Romans to

   _____ .

7. Before going to Spain Paul had to deliver a

   _____ to _____ .

8. The collection had two purposes. One was to provide
   _____ for the poor in Jerusalem. A second
   purpose was to unify _____ and

   _____ .

9. Paul asks the Romans to pray that the collection will be
   properly accepted by

   _____ .

10. Paul asks the Romans to pray that he will be protected
against _____.

(Check your answers on page 193.)

RIGHTEOUS
THROUGH FAITH

Righteous Through Faith:
A Study of the Epistle to the Romans

SECTION EIGHT:
Conclusion of the Letter (Romans 16:1-27)

Praise for a Deaconess (Romans 16:1,2)

(Read Romans 16:1,2)

> [1] I would like you to welcome our sister Phoebe. She serves the church in Cenchrea. [2] I ask you to receive her as one who belongs to the Lord. Receive her in the way God's people should. Give her any help she may need from you. She has been a great help to many people, including me.

Paul asks the Romans to welcome Sister Phoebe. We are not told what work she did for the church in Cenchrea, or why she is now going to Rome. Since she is described as serving the church, it is more likely that she is a deaconess than a blood relative. She has been helpful to many people, including Paul. In fact, she may be providing him with special service in connection with this trip to Rome.

Keep in mind that Paul wrote this letter from the Greek city of Corinth. It was located on a narrow neck of land, with sea on both sides. It had two harbors, one facing west; the other to the east. Cenchrea was the eastern-facing harbor.

In the ancient world there was no international mail service such as we take for granted today. If you wanted to send a letter to someone, the best procedure was to find someone who was traveling to that place and have them personally deliver your letter. It is quite possible that Phoebe is the carrier delivering Paul's letter to the Romans. The letter may also have served as a letter of introduction for her.

Things to remember:

1. Phoebe is from the Greek city of _____,
   which is also the city from which Paul is writing.
2. Phoebe, traveling to the city of _____, may be
   carrying _____ _____.

(Check your answers on page 186.)

Greetings from Paul (Romans 16:3-16)

(Read Romans 16:3-5)

³ Greet Priscilla and Aquila. They work together with me in serving
Christ Jesus. ⁴ They have put their lives in danger for me. I am thankful
for them. So are all the non-Jewish churches.
⁵ Greet also the church that meets in the house of Priscilla and Aquila.

Acts 18:1-3 informs us that Aquila and Pricilla were a
husband and wife team. Paul met them on his first visit to
Corinth. They were tent-makers, as Paul was, so he worked
with them for a while to support his ministry. Aquila and
Priscilla traveled about to many cities and took the Christian
message wherever they went. At the time of Paul's writing
this letter they were in Rome, where Paul sends greetings to
them.

This pious couple had assembled a Christian
congregation that was meeting in their home. The early
Christian congregations were "house churches." They did not
have the means to build separate "church" buildings. Nor
would it have been wise to draw attention (and persecution)
to themselves by constructing elaborate places of worship.
Perhaps even this low-profile house church activity was risky
for them. Paul says of Aquila and Priscilla, "They have put
their lives in danger."

Things to remember:

3. _____ and _____ were a
   husband and wife team that Paul first met in Corinth.
4. Their occupation was _____ _____ but
   they were also very good missionaries.
5. In Rome they had a Christian congregation meeting in

   _____ _____.

(Check your answers on page 186.)

This next section of the letter is a listing of the various people to whom the apostle is sending personal greetings. The readers in Rome will have recognized immediately who was referred to. We are not so fortunate. None of the people named here is mentioned anywhere else in Scripture. Our knowledge is limited to the bits of information Paul adds to the individual names.

Perhaps the most workable approach is to read the whole list and then to come back and see what connections and groupings can be made.

(Read Romans 16:5-16)

> Greet my dear friend Epenetus. He was the first person in Asia Minor to become a believer in Christ.
> [6] Greet Mary. She worked very hard for you.
> [7] Greet Andronicus and Junias, my relatives. They have been in prison with me. They are leaders among the apostles. They became believers in Christ before I did.
> [8] Greet Ampliatus. I love him as a brother in the Lord.
> [9] Greet Urbanus. He works together with me in serving Christ. And greet my dear friend Stachys.
> [10] Greet Apelles. Even though he was put to the test, he remained faithful as one who belonged to Christ.
> Greet those who live in the house of Aristobulus.
> [11] Greet Herodion, my relative.
> Greet the believers who live in the house of Narcissus.
> [12] Greet Tryphena and Tryphosa. Those women work hard for the Lord.
> Greet my dear friend Persis. She is another woman who has worked

very hard for the Lord.
[13] Greet Rufus. He is a choice believer in the Lord. And greet his mother. She has been like a mother to me too.
[14] Greet Asyncritus, Phlegon and Hermes. Greet Patrobas, Hermas and the believers with them.
[15] Greet Philologus, Julia, Nereus and his sister. Greet Olympas and all of God's people with them.
[16] Greet one another with a holy kiss.
All the churches of Christ send their greetings.

The first thing to note is how long the list is. Paul sends greetings by name to more than twenty people. There is no list like it in any other letter of Scripture. This large number is the more remarkable when we remember that Paul has not visited the congregation in Rome. A possible explanation is that Paul got to know them earlier while he was working in the area "from Jerusalem…to Illyricum" and they have since that time moved to Rome. For example, verse 5 shares the information that Epenetus "was the first person in Asia Minor to become a Christian."

A second item of interest is the number of women greeted and commended in the list. Paul himself remained unmarried and in his first letter to the Corinthians he advises that in troubled times it might be advisable for other people to remain single also. Some have misunderstood this, as thought he was a woman-hater. But note the cordial greeting by name and the glowing praise he includes for seven women:

Greet Mary. She worked very hard for you. (v 6)
Greet Tryphena and Tryphosa. Those women work hard for the Lord. (12)
Greet my dear friend Persis. She is another woman who has worked very hard for the Lord. (12)
Greet Rufus…and his mother. She has been like a mother to me too. (13)
Greet… Julia… and [Nereus] sister. (15)

Paul closes the list by urging his readers, "Greet one another with a holy kiss." This was an indication of the unity that existed in their Christian group. It was a visible expression of the faith they shared. It did not have any romantic implications.

Things to remember:
6. The letter to the Romans has an unusually long list of

    _____.

7. We can tell Paul is not a _____

    _____ by his praise of women.

8. The holy kiss Paul urges was an expression of

    _____.

(Check your answers on page 186.)

A Warning

(Read Romans 16:17-20)

[17] I am warning you, brothers and sisters, to watch out for those who try to keep you from staying together. They want to trip you up. They teach you things opposite to what you have learned. Stay away from them. [18] People like that are not serving Christ our Lord. They are serving only themselves. With smooth talk and with words they don't mean they fool people who don't know any better.

[19] Everyone has heard that you obey God. So you have filled me with joy. I want you to be wise about what is good. And I want you to have nothing to do with what is evil.

[20] The God who gives peace will soon crush Satan under your feet.
May the grace of our Lord Jesus be with you.

Paul has sent greetings to over twenty individuals, as well as to some groups of believers who gather in private homes. But there is one group he does not greet. They are the false teachers who are bothering the Roman Christians

Paul previously urged the strong believers to be considerate of those who were weak in faith. These weaker members were people who were unclear about some spiritually neutral things. Examples Paul mentioned included

Jesus sends out his disciples.

misunderstandings some people had about what foods to eat or about the proper day on which to worship. As long as the discussion remains about neutral things, and the weaker members remain willing to learn, they are to be treated with great consideration and patience.

But the situation changes completely if a weaker brother is no longer willing to listen and learn. Instead he sets himself up as a teacher and insists the thing in question is not neutral but a requirement for salvation. That is not to be tolerated.

A similar problem occurs when something that is not neutral is treated as if it were. One of the things that never is neutral is the doctrine taught in the Bible. Jesus sent the apostles out to preach the gospel to all people, "teaching them to obey everything I have commanded you" (Matthew 28:20). Correct teaching is essential!

Paul does not tell the Romans, "A little false doctrine won't hurt you." Paul is very clear in how they are to deal with false teachers. He says, "Stay away from them!" False teachers are dangerous! "They want to trip you up. They teach you things opposite to what you have learned....People like that are not serving Christ our Lord. They are serving only themselves."

Paul's motive for speaking so strongly is not hostility toward false teachers. Rather, it is love for simple believers whom he is trying to protect. He tells them "I want you to be wise about what is good. And I want you to have nothing to do with what is evil."

False teachers can be appealing and deceptive. Paul says of them, "With smooth talk and with words they don't mean they fool people who don't know any better." False teachers are dangerous but the believers in Rome are not defenseless. They (and we too) have the Word through which the Holy Spirit works. Armed with this Paul can confidently promise, "The God who gives peace will soon crush Satan under your feet."

Things to remember:

9. Paul sends greetings to many people in Rome, but there is one group he does not greet. Instead of greeting them he warns against _____ _____.

10. The Romans are urged to _____ false teachers.

11. False teachers are dangerous because they teach things _____ to what the believers had learned before.

12. False teachers are not serving _____. They are serving _____.

13. We learn correct doctrine by studying _____

_____.

(Check your answers on page 186.)

Greetings from Paul's Co-workers

(Read Romans 16:21-24)

[21] Timothy works together with me. He sends his greetings to you. So do Lucius, Jason and Sosipater, my relatives.

[22] I, Tertius, wrote down this letter. I greet you as a believer in the Lord.

[23-24] Gaius sends you his greetings. He has welcomed me and the whole church here into his house.

Erastus is the director of public works here in the city. He sends you his greetings. Our brother Quartus also greets you.

Acts 16:1-3 informs us that on his second mission journey Paul made the acquaintance of a young man named Timothy. Recognizing his special talents for doing mission work, Paul took him along when he continued on his mission journey.

Previously in speaking of Paul's outreach method we noted that Paul started congregations in major urban centers and then moved on to other places. Meanwhile he left behind co-workers to serve those congregations and to reach out with the gospel in the surrounding neighborhood. Timothy was among those co-workers. At this time he is with Paul in Corinth. On other occasions he served alone. Two of Paul's letters to him are included among the New Testament books.

Of Lucius, Jason and Sosipater we know nothing other than their names and the fascinating detail that they are "relatives" of Paul. The situation becomes even more interesting when we recall that the list of people in Rome whom Paul greeted earlier in this chapter also included three "relatives"—Andronicus and Junias (v. 7) and Herodion (v. 11). In the case of Andronicus and Junias Paul adds the intriguing detail, "They became believers in Christ before I did." That seems to suggest that while Saul/Paul was ferociously persecuting Christians, some of his family members were being won for the faith.

Printing did not become a standard practice until the 1400s. Before that time everything had to be copied by hand. A very important occupation was being a professional secretary. Paul apparently dictated this letter and Tertius, a Christian brother, wrote his words down in good handwriting.

Gaius was a fairly common name in ancient times. The name turns up several times in New Testament letters, but we do not know if it is the same person who is sending greetings here. Note another example of the early Christians meeting in private homes, rather than in public places of worship.

Both the book of Acts and Paul's second letter to Timothy make mention of a co-worker named Erastus. Those passages indicate that this Erastus was actively engaged in doing mission work. The man here sending his greetings to acquaintances in Rome seems to have been a rather high ranking city official in Corinth, so perhaps he is not the same as Paul's missionary helper.

Quartus is mentioned only here in Scripture.

Things to remember:

14. Timothy was one of Paul's _____.

15. Tertius was Paul's _____.
16. Erastus was a _____ _____ in
    Corinth.
(Check your answers on page 186.)

(Read Romans 16:25-27)

[25] May God receive glory. He is able to strengthen your faith because of the good news I preach. It is the message about Jesus Christ. It is in keeping with the mystery that was hidden for a very long time. [26] The mystery has now been made known through the writings of the prophets. The eternal God commanded that it be made known. He wanted all nations to believe and obey him. [27] May the only wise God receive glory forever through Jesus Christ. Amen.

Paul ends his letter as he began it. He directs the readers' attention to the saving gospel message he has been called to preach. In verse 16 of the opening chapter he stated, "I am not ashamed of the good news. It is God's power. And it will save everyone who believes. It is meant first for the Jews. It is meant also for those who aren't Jews."

Here in the closing paragraph of his letter Paul once more calls attention to the greatness of his message. He assures his readers that his message is all they need. He tells them, "God …is able to strengthen your faith because of the good news I preach. It is the message about Jesus Christ."

Throughout the ages there has always been only one plan of salvation. It is by faith in Jesus Christ, the promised Messiah. Because this promised Savior was to be born of the Jewish nation, God gave them special rules and regulations. To many people that seemed to indicate that God's plan of salvation was only for the Jewish nation. That all nations, Gentiles as well as Jews, were the objects of God's saving love was a "mystery" that needed to be explained to the world.

God's calling Paul as a missionary to the Gentiles made

Jesus speaks with Nicodemus.

perfectly clear what he had intended from the very beginning. Paul states, "The eternal God commanded that it (the mystery) be made known. He wanted all nations to believe and obey him."

This message of God's grace to all nations was proclaimed already by the Old Testament prophets. It was preserved in their writings, but it needed to be explained to the New Testament world. Paul's letter to the Romans provides a masterful explanation of God's saving plan. It is a plan that provides righteousness for both Jews and Gentiles through the merit of Jesus Christ. By faith the believer accepts Christ's righteousness as his own.

Covered by Christ's righteousness, the forgiven sinner can now stand before a just and holy God.

Understanding and accepting this message of salvation as a free gift was absolutely essential for the Romans. But it remains equally important also for us. Although we live 2000 years later and far from Rome, by God's grace Paul's letter has reached us also. Let us cherish its message and accept it for what it is, the power of God for the salvation of all who believe.

For so precious a gift we can only respond, as the apostle does, with words of awe and praise. "May the only wise God receive glory forever through Jesus Christ. Amen."

Things to remember:

17. In both the Old and New Testaments, there is only _____ plan of salvation.

18. That salvation comes to the sinner by faith in _____.

19. By faith Christ's _____ is credited to the _____.

20. Covered by Christ's _____, the believer can now stand before _____ without fear.

21. The believer in Christ can be sure of spending eternity
    with _____ in _____ .
(Check your answers on page 186.)

Things to remember-Answers

1. Corinth; 2. Rome, Paul's letter; 3. Aquila, Priscilla; 4. tent making;
5. their home; 6. greetings; 7. woman hater; 8. unity among believers;
9. false teachers; 10. stay away from; 11. opposite; 12. Christ, themselves;
13. the Bible; 14. co-workers; 15. secretary; 16. city official; 17. one;
18. Christ; 19. righteousness, believer; 20. righteousness, God;
21. God, heaven.

TEST - Righteous Through Faith: A Study of the Epistle to the Romans

Section 8

Please review the "Things to remember."

---

1. Phoebe was from the Greek city of _____.
   She may be carrying _____.

2. _____ and _____ were a
   husband and wife team. Their occupation was
   _____ _____ but they were also
   very good _____.

3. The letter to the Romans has an unusually long list of
   _____.

4. The holy kiss Paul urges was an expression of
   _____.

5. Instead of greeting them, Paul rather warns against
   _____ _____.

6. The Romans are urged to _____
   false teachers.

7. False teachers are not serving _____. They
   are serving _____.

8. We learn correct doctrine by studying _____ _____.

9. Tertius was Paul's _____.

10. In both the Old and New Testaments, there is only
    _____ plan of salvation.

11. By faith Christ's _____ is credited to the _____.

12. Covered by Christ's _____, the believer can stand before _____ without fear.

13. The believer in Christ can be sure of spending eternity with _____ in _____.

(Check your answers on page 193.)

GLOSSARY
Righteous Through Faith:
A Study of the Epistle to the Romans

Abba – A name for God used in the New Testament that meant "father." It is a name children use for their fathers which shows a close family relationship and respect.

Circumcision – The act of cutting off the foreskin of the male. In the Old Testament it was the sign and seal of God's covenant promise of salvation to Israel which began with Abraham. It is the mark that said these people belong to God. In the New Testament, believers enter the church through Baptism into faith and a new life in Christ.

Conscience – The inborn knowledge that there is a God and that certain things are right and certain things are wrong according to the law of God. Our conscience tells us that, according to the law, good actions merit his approval and reward, and bad actions deserve his anger and condemnation.

Conversion – Turning to God, through faith in Jesus, by the gracious power of the Holy Spirit. It includes both turning away from sin (repentance in the narrow sense) and turning to Jesus by faith. The Holy Spirit works conversion in sinners through the gospel found in God's Word and in the sacraments of Baptism and the Lord's Supper.

Covenant – 1) The divine covenant of grace is God's solemn promise to enter into a relationship with his people and to bless them, based on his promise of a Savior. It is a one-sided or unilateral covenant since it is entirely the gracious work of God, begun and completed by him for our salvation. 2) A covenant may also be two-sided or bilateral. In the law covenant that was given to Moses on Mount Sinai, both parties promised to enter into a relationship with and do something for each other.

Covet – To want something you should not have, because it is against God's will and command. To covet is to continue to want something you cannot rightly get, because it is beyond your ability to do so.

Easter – The church festival that celebrates Jesus' resurrection or rising from the dead. Easter usually refers to the time Jesus bodily came back to life on the third day, the Sunday after he died on Good Friday.

Gay – A person, male or female who is a homosexual and has sexual relationships with a person of their own gender, a woman with a woman or a man with a man.

Glorify – It means to praise and honor God.

Glorified body – A body given to believers in heaven that is like Jesus' body after he rose from the dead. It will be a perfect body.

Grace – The favor or undeserved love of God that gives salvation to condemned sinners as a free gift. Grace also gives believers the spiritual gifts they need to serve God.

Homosexuality – The sin of having sexual relations with a person of one's own sex. It is condemned in God's Word as a perversion of the natural order.

Hypocrisy - The practice of a person who pretends to be something he or she is not. The act of saying that he or she believes in Jesus, or tries to act like he or she loves him, but really does not.

Innocent – A person who is not guilty of committing a sin or a crime. Jesus did not sin, he was innocent. Jesus was not guilty of the charges the Jews brought against him at his trial before Pontius Pilate. To be innocent means to be "not guilty."

Inspiration - The work of the Holy Spirit in the hearts and minds of the authors of the Bible. The Holy Spirit prepared and guided the writers so that every word they wrote was the Word of God. The purpose was so people would know God and his way of salvation. "Inspiration" is taken from the word meaning "God-breathed" in 2 Timothy 3:16.

Merit – It is a good standing earned by doing something good. Jesus lived a perfect life and died an innocent death in our place and thus merited, for us, our salvation and made us right with God.

Orthodox – It is a true or right belief. It is the true and official teachings of a church based on the true Word of God. These teachings are the standard for judging everything that is taught and done in the church. It is commonly accepted that it is true and right.

Pagan – A person who worships false gods, many gods, or the spirits they believe to be in nature.

Penitent – Someone who is sorry for his or her sins and believes in Jesus as the Savior.

Pious – Having or showing strong religious feelings, reverence for God.

Redeemed – To buy back. Being set free, rescued or delivered from slavery. It is related to ransom, paying the price to release a slave or prisoner. It is the means whereby a sinner is saved.

Repent – To be sorry for sin and turning away from it including turning to God for forgiveness, through faith in Jesus. Then a person will want to live a new, holy life.

Righteousness – Doing what is right and good, holy and pure. It is used in different ways. God is perfectly righteous and holy. His law is perfect and he does what is pure, right and good. God declares believers to be righteous in his sight (justification). He transfers the standing of Christ, objectively to all people, subjectively to all believers. Believers are commanded to live righteous lives. They do this with the help of the Holy Spirit.

Sacred – Religious in nature or use, holy by being connected with God.

Substitute – One who takes the place of and acts for another. Jesus took our place in life and death to earn righteousness and eternal life for us sinners.

Synagogue – The Jewish house of worship, prayer and teaching. There were many synagogues but only one Temple. It was different from the Temple because there were no sacrifices or priestly services in the synagogue. Most people believe the synagogues began during the time the Jews were away from the Temple, in Babylon.

Temptation – It has two related meanings. 1) Satan tries to lead people to sin. God never tempts a person to sin. 2) It also means a trial, testing a person, to show where they are strong or weak and to strengthen their faith. God does this is several ways.

ANSWERS to Section Tests
Righteous Through Faith:
A Study of the Epistle to the Romans

Section 1: (pages 13-14)
1. Saul, Paul; 2. dangerous, destroyed; 3. persecuting;
4. apostle; 5. savior; 6. Jesus, Mary, human; 7. Holy Spirit, God;
8. Gentiles; 9. visit; 10. preach; 11. righteousness; 12. sinners;
13. righteous; 14. faith.

Section 2: (pages 32-33)
1. the created world; 2. obedience; 3. sinning; 4. same-gender;
5. die; 6. encourage; 7. repent; 8. good works, faith; 9. gift;
10. Gentiles, hearts; 11. conscience, sinning; 12. special;
13. agreement, Jesus; 14. the Old Testament Bible; 15. expects of
people, save them; 16. show us our need for a savior.

Section 3: (pages 55-56)
1. Everyone, die; 2. died, sins, forgive; 3. anything, believing;
4. through; 5. before, faith; 6. land, many descendents, a Savior
from sin; 7. faith; 8. dead, trust; 9. our, faith; 10. raised;
11. peace, joy, God, heaven; 12. faith; 13. Holy Spirit, gives;
14. enemies, Christ; 15. death, inherited; 16. everyone, earn,
salvation.

Section 4: (pages 91-92)
1. faith, Christ; 2. sin, bad things, pleases; 3. God; 4. sin, Savior;
5. new man, good things; 6. sinful, "old Adam"; 7. fight;
8. offering; 9. forgiveness; 10. Triune, three, one; 11. raise, live;
12. trust, confidence, promises; 13. Holy Spirit, heavenly Father;
14. eternity; 15. believe; 16. glorify us in heaven; 17. no one.

Section 5: (page120)
1. Believe in Christ; 2. Jews, special people; 3. Gentiles; 4. earn,
works, gift; 5. Gentiles, Jews; 6. Jewish nation; 7. Gentiles; 8.
mercy, Jews, Gentiles.

Section 6: (pages 154-155)
1. mercy; 2. sacrifices; 3. gifts, thank, people; 4. Christians, non-Christians; 5. evil, peace; 6. God, evil, good; 7. heart, actions; 8. love; 9. Saturday, any day; 10. faith; 11. sin, God; 12. wrong; 13. Christ; 14. Bible; 15. servant; 16. Old Testament prophets.

Section 7: (pages 170-171)
1. offerings; 2. Gentile Christians; 3. urban, the surrounding countryside; 4. Spain; 5. visit the Romans; 6. support his mission work in Spain; 7. collection, poor Christians in Jerusalem; 8. relief, Jews, Gentiles; 9. Jewish Christians in Jerusalem; 10. unbelieving Jews in Jerusalem.

Section 8: (pages 187-188)
1. Corinth, Paul's letter; 2. Aquila, Pricilla, tent making, missionaries; 3. greetings; 4. unity among Christians; 5. false teachers; 6. stay away from; 7. Christ, themselves; 8. the Bible; 9. secretary; 10. one; 11. righteousness, believer; 12. righteousness, God; 13. God, heaven.

FINAL TEST
Righteous Through Faith:
A Study of the Epistle to the Romans

Go back through the book and review any mistakes you made in the section tests. Then complete the final test without looking at the book. When you have finished, give the test to the person who gave you this book or mail the test to the place listed on the back of this book.

Words needed to complete each question are listed at the end of the test.

Righteous Through Faith

1. The author of the letter to the Romans first had the name _____ but he changed it to _____.

2. Saul thought Christians were _____ and should be _____.

3. On the road to Damascus Jesus met Saul and said to him "Why are you_____ me?"

4. Jesus appointed Saul to be an _____.

5. Paul did not start the congregation in Rome but he very much wanted to _____ them.

6. After the fall into sin God promised Eve that from her descendants a _____ would be born.

7. This promised "Seed of the woman" was _____ who was born of _____. Hence Jesus is truly _____.

8. Jesus had no earthly father. He was born by the power of the _____ _____. Thus he is also true _____.

9. God is patient with sinners in order to give them time to _____.

10. Salvation is not earned by doing _____. It comes through _____ in what Christ has done.

11. By nature, people have a _____. When they go against their conscience they are _____.

12. God's law tells us what God _____.
    Because sinners can't keep the law, the law can't

    _____ _____.

13. We are not saved because of faith but _____
    faith.

14. Abraham was saved through faith _____ he
    was circumcised and not after. Only _____
    saves; not anything we do.

15. God made a three-fold promise to Abraham. He
    promised him:
    a)_____ ,
    b)_____ , and
    c)_____.

16. Abraham and Sarah could be considered _____ as
    far as child-bearing was concerned. Even so, Abraham
    continued to _____ God's promises.

17. God the Father _____ Jesus from death to prove
    that he was satisfied with Jesus' sacrifice for the
    world's sin.

18. With our sins forgiven we have _____ with
    God. When there is peace with God, there is also
    _____. This joy looks forward to spending
    eternity with _____ in _____.

19. Suffering and hardship strengthen our

    _____.

20. When we were _____ of God _____ died to make us friends of God.

21. Christ's sacrifice earned righteousness for _____. Some people don't believe that. They think they can _____ righteousness by what they do. Such people will not receive God's gift of _____.

22. With Christ we died to _____ in our baptism. We will now try to avoid doing _____ and we will try to do what _____ God.

23. The law is good because it shows us our _____ and our need for a _____ from sin.

24. Coming to faith gives the believer a _____ _____. This new man wants to do _____ _____.

25. Every believer still has a _____ nature. This sinful nature is often called our _____ _____.

26. Every day the "new man" and the "old Adam" _____ with each other

27. Christ's death earned _____ for the sins of the whole world.

28. The God of the Bible is a _____ God. This means there are _____ persons in _____ God.

29. On judgment day God will _____ those
    who have died. Believers will _____
    forever with God in heaven.

30. When our prayer life is weak, the _____
    _____ helps us. Such prayers are acceptable
    to our _____.

31. From _____ God planned our salvation.

32. God's promises to the Jewish nation are still good. But
    many Jews are missing out on salvation because they
    want to _____ it by their own _____
    rather than accept it as a _____ from
    God.

33. In New Testament times God gave his blessings to the
    _____ in order to make the
    _____ jealous. God hoped that Jews also
    would accept his salvation.

34. In biblical language a "mystery" is something that has
    to be explained to people. The mystery Paul explains in
    chapter 11 is how God has shown _____ to both
    _____ and _____.

35. Each of us has received _____ from
    God. Believers use their gifts to _____ God
    and to serve _____.

36. Rulers and authorities are placed over us by
    _____. Rulers are called to
    punish those who do _____ and to reward
    those who do_____.

37. When obeying rulers, the attitude of our _____ is just as important as our outward _____.

38. The central requirement of all the Commandments is to _____.

39. Paul warns strong Christians not to do anything that would harm the _____ of a weaker brother.

40. Saving Gentiles was not an idea that began in the New Testament. It was foretold already by the _____.

41. Paul shares his plan to go to the country of _____. On his way there he wants to _____.

42. Paul invites the Romans to _____.

43. Before going to Spain Paul had to deliver a collection to the city of _____. The collection had two purposes. One was to provide _____ for poor Christians in Jerusalem. A second purpose was to unify _____ and _____.

44. _____ and _____ were a husband and wife team. Their occupation was _____ _____ but they were also very good _____.

45. The letter to the Romans has an unusually long list of _____.

46. The holy kiss Paul urges was an expression of _____.

47. The Romans are urged to _____
    false teachers. False teachers are not serving
    _____. They are serving _____.

48. By faith Christ's _____ is credited to
    _____.

49. Covered by Christ's _____, believers can
    stand before _____ without fear.

50. The believer in Christ can be sure of spending eternity
    with _____ in _____.

Answers needed to complete the final test.

actions	God
apostle	God
Aquila	God
bad things	good
before	good things
believers	good works
Christ	greetings
Christ	heart
conscience	heaven
dangerous	heaven
dead	heavenly Father
destroyed	Holy Spirit
earn	Holy Spirit
earn	human
enemies	Jerusalem
eternity	Jesus
everyone	Jews
evil	Jews
expects of people	Jews
faith	joy
faith	land
faith	live
faith	love
fight	many descendants
forgiveness	Mary
Gentiles	mercy
Gentiles	missionaries
Gentiles	new man
gift	old Adam
gifts	Old Testament
God	prophets
God	one

Paul
peace
people
persecuting
pleases
Priscilla
raise
raised
relief
repent
righteousness
righteousness
salvation
Saul
save them
Savior
Savior
Savior from sin
sin

sin
sinful
sinning
Spain
stay away from
support his mission
      work in Spain
tent making
thank
themselves
three
through
Triune
trust
unity among Christians
visit
visit the Romans
works

Please PRINT the following information.

NAME: _____

ADDRESS: _____

_____

_____

Please give us your comments on this course.

_____

_____

_____

_____

_____

_____